J. F. Bransford

Archæological Researches in Nicaragua

J. F. Bransford

Archæological Researches in Nicaragua

ISBN/EAN: 9783337059903

Printed in Europe, USA, Canada, Australia, Japan

Cover: Foto ©ninafisch / pixelio.de

More available books at **www.hansebooks.com**

SMITHSONIAN CONTRIBUTIONS TO KNOWLEDGE.
— 383 —

ARCHÆOLOGICAL RESEARCHES

IN

NICARAGUA.

BY

J. F. BRANSFORD, M. D.,
PASSED ASSISTANT SURGEON, U. S. NAVY.

WASHINGTON CITY:
PUBLISHED BY THE SMITHSONIAN INSTITUTION.
1881.

ADVERTISEMENT.

The following memoir gives an account of a large and interesting archæological collection made by Dr. Bransford while detailed as a medical officer to accompany the expeditions under Commander Lull, United States Navy, which visited Nicaragua and Costa Rica to make surveys for an inter-oceanic ship-canal, and during two subsequent visits, under the order of the Navy Department, to the same region for the purpose of obtaining additional data for the same object.

This collection comprising 788 articles, deposited in the National Museum, is particularly valuable since all the objects, with the exception of a few obtained by purchase, were dug up by the author and the exact position in which each was found carefully noted.

The memoir gives the first satisfactory account of the peculiar form of burial—in urns—practiced on the island of Ometepec; for while the urns themselves have been previously mentioned, their use as coffins has never before been fully described. A description is also given of some mounds, stone graves, images, rock inscriptions, and pottery believed to be distinctively Mexican in form.

The thanks of the Institution are due to Mr. Ran. Runnels, Dr. Adan Cardenas, and Señor Don José Chamorro, for valuable assistance rendered the author in his investigations.

The paper was furnished to the Institution in December, 1878, but the author's absence on a cruise to Asia prevented its publication until the present time.

SPENCER F. BAIRD,
Secretary of the Smithsonian Institution.

SMITHSONIAN INSTITUTION,
WASHINGTON, D. C., *January,* 1881.

CONTENTS.

Preliminary Notice . . . . Page	1
Introduction	3
CHAPTER I.—Ometepec	5
Urn Burial	7
Luna Pottery	20
Contents of Urns	44
Hacienda de Baltaza	46
Chilaite	47
CHAPTER II.—Pueblo Viejo	49
Santa Helena	50
CHAPTER III.—Stone Graves	59
Mounds	60
Stone Images	62
Rock Carvings	64
CHAPTER IV.—Palmar	69
Managua	70
San Juan del Sur	70
Manufacture of Pottery near San Jorge	71
CHAPTER V.—Nicoya	73
CHAPTER VI.—Conclusion	79
CATALOGUE OF COLLECTION	85

PRELIMINARY NOTICE.

In December, 1872, the Navy Department sent an expedition under Commander E. P. Lull, U. S. N., to Nicaragua to complete the surveys begun in the spring of the same year for an inter-oceanic ship canal.*

I accompanied the expedition as medical officer, with instructions to make general scientific investigations in the natural history, &c., of the country. The island of Ometepec was visited, and while hunting for antiquities I chanced to see a ditch which had been recently dug, and in which burial urns were exposed *in situ*. This was on a hacienda belonging to Don José Angel Luna, near Moyogalpa.

In 1876 I was sent to Nicaragua on special duty connected with the survey, and was instructed to make archæological investigations on the island of Ometepec. I was in the country from January until the middle of May, more than half the time exploring and excavating on the island, the principal portion of the work being done at Luna's, Los Angeles, and San Francisco.

Again, in February, 1877, I went down and remained until the first of July. As before, most of the time was spent on the island, paying attention chiefly to the neighborhood of Santa Helena and Chilaite, north of Moyogalpa. Then some investigations were made on the mainland near San Jorge, followed by a trip into Costa Rica, as far south as Nicoya.

On both the later expeditions I had aid from the Smithsonian Institution, including an outfit for collecting and preserving natural history specimens.†

The material for this paper has been taken from the reports made to the Navy Department in 1876 and 1877, and from the collections obtained and deposited in the National Museum.

J. F. BRANSFORD.

U. S. S. RICHMOND, BOSTON, *Dec.* 20, 1878.

---

* For valuable information concerning the country see the report published by the Navy Department, 1874, on Surveys for a Ship Canal through Nicaragua.

† For an account of a collection of fish from Lake Nicaragua see paper in Proceedings Academy Natural Sciences, Philadelphia, July, 1877.

INTRODUCTION.

The continuation of the main mountain range of North America, in passing through Nicaragua, divides the republic into two nearly equal sections. Bending more to the south in Costa Rica, and branching out, it encloses the elevated table lands of San José and Cartago. These mountains attain a height of 3,000 to 4,000 feet in Nicaragua, and in Costa Rica reach an extreme altitude of 10,850 feet in the volcano of Cartago.* The Atlantic slope of the Cordillera, which condenses the moisture of the trade wind, is clothed with dense vegetation, while on the Pacific side the climate is less damp, and the wet and dry seasons are well defined.

South of the bay of Realejo a chain of hills appears and follows the coast in a general southwest direction to Capo Blanco, Costa Rica. The elevation does not anywhere exceed 2,000 feet.

Between the two mountain ridges lies a plain, from the gulf of Fonseca to the Nicaragua lake basin, which, in turn, extends to the valley of the Rio Frio. A southwest extension of the plain, between the volcano Orosi and the ocean, rises into a table land of a thousand feet elevation,† on which are the head-waters of the Sapoa and Tempisque rivers. The former empties into Lake Nicaragua, and the latter into the head of the gulf of Nicoya.

The middle section of this long valley, the Nicaragua lake basin, contains the two great lakes of Managua and Nicaragua. They seem originally to have formed a portion of a bay of the Pacific, and, later, to have been cut off from the ocean by upheaval of the land south of Fonseca. The surplus water of Lake Nicaragua is discharged by the San Juan River into the Atlantic, the river finding its way in a succession of rapids through the main range of mountains.

A series of volcanoes leaves the Cordillera at its bend in Costa Rica, and keeps an almost direct line from Orosi to Fonseca. The peaks rise at intervals along the lake and plain, reaching an altitude of 6,266 feet in El Viejo,‡ the highest in the Nicaragua section.

---

* Nicaragua. P. Levy, pp. 76, 80.
† Reports of Explorations and Surveys for the Location of a Ship Canal between the Atlantic and Pacific Oceans, through Nicaragua, 1872-'73. Washington, 1874.
‡ Nicaragua. P. Levy, p. 84.

INTRODUCTION.

Repeated and glowing descriptions have been given of the beauty of the scenery and the fertility of the soil of the Pacific slope of Nicaragua, while the little known valley of the Tempisque and the region around the gulf of Nicoya are hardly inferior to it in either respect. The Spanish conquerors found both sections occupied by large populations engaged in the pursuit of peaceful arts and industries. Dr. Berendt, a great explorer and student of the ancient inhabitants of Central America, in the light of the philological results obtained by Squier and himself, and of the traditions preserved especially by Oviedo, Herrera, and Torquemada, believed that the Cholutecas, Chorotegas, Dirians, and Orotiñans were descendants of people who emigrated from Cholula, Mexico. These people possessed the major portion of the country from Fonseca to Nicoya, their territorial continuity being interrupted in the neighborhood of the present Leon by the Marabios, and again by an Aztec colony occupying the narrowest part of the belt between the Pacific and Lake Nicaragua, and the islands of the lake. The king and the capital of the latter nation bore the name of Nicarao.[*] The ancient inhabitants of this whole region left abundant relics of their civilization in mounds, burial places, &c.

The antiquities so far discovered in Nicaragua have been almost all on the Pacific slope, where the conditions are more favorable for the development of large populations.

---

[*] Address read before the American Geographical Society, July 10th, 1876, by Dr. C. H. Berendt.

CHAPTER I.

OMETEPEC.

Opposite Rivas, and about eight miles from the west coast of Lake Nicaragua, is the island of Ometepec, some twenty miles long by nine wide. Its length is in the same general direction as that of the lake, northwest. It is formed by two extinct volcanoes, Ometepec and Madera, between which is a strip of lowland said to be occasionally overflowed by the high water of the rainy season. The geological formation is, of course, volcanic; enormous blocks of basalt in some places cover the mountain side, while near the lake, on the northern or Ometepec end, there is quite level land, extending at some points as far as two miles inland, and extremely fertile.

Of the mountains, Madera has the more aged appearance, with rugged outline and ridged and shaggy sides. Dense forests cover it, except where the rock shows in a few grim patches. There is very little arable land on this end of the island, the inhabitants being confined to a few favorable spots near the lake shore. There is a beautiful stream down the north side of the mountain, which, with two small ones in the level connecting slip, constitutes the only running water on the island during the dry season.

The volcano Ometepec, according to my aneroid, is 4,550 feet high, some four or five hundred feet more elevated than Madera. It is very regular in outline; in form, the model volcano. Its gracefully sloping sides fall with less abruptness as the lake is approached, until a tolerably level plain on the northeast and another on the southwest form, respectively, the districts of Alta Gracia and Moyogalpa. This mountain also is well wooded to the top, except on the southwest side, where, about a third of the way down from the summit, the timber abruptly terminates, and grass llanos spread down towards the shore. The southwest side of the crater seems to have been blown out by one of the later eruptions, and a depression near the middle of the remaining portion of the rim gives the two points to the peak. An enormous gulch extends from the blown-out side of the crater half way down the mountain, bounding the llanos on the south. The latter are on a formation of ash, cinder, and lava, the results of the last eruptions. The cinder, and in some places the lava, overlies the ash, and has on the surface just enough of soil to support a magnificent growth of

(5)

grass. The llanos widen as they descend, until, in the foot hills, they extend from Moyogalpa on the north to Los Angeles, south. Near the lake, around these villages and between them, is a tract of arable land of unsurpassed fertility. The recent formation, which encroaches on the lake between the villages, is of alternate layers of volcanic ash and caked cinder, or rotten lava of a loose formation, with a rich soil on the surface. A section exposed in a bank above the beach at the hacienda de Baltaza shows in twelve feet two layers of cinder and four of ash.

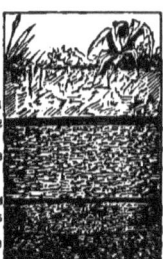

Section, hacienda de Baltaza.

On this end of the island there are no streams, the porous ground absorbing all the rain-fall, except in the wet season. Still vegetation, especially on the southwest side, is kept green by the showers which almost daily come down the mountain. In the driest season the peak draws an unfailing supply from the trade wind.

Cacao grows here with great luxuriance, and the planter can choose for his crop sugar, coffee, rice, cotton, or indigo, with all the fruits of tropical America. But the favorite productions are watermelons and tobacco, which grow better than elsewhere in the republic.

The inhabitants of the island are said to number three thousand, the majority of whom live in or near Alta Gracia. Of the rest some five or six hundred are at Moyogalpa and the others scattered over the island; fifteen or twenty houses constituting the village of Los Angeles, and a few families living on the Madera end. Most of the people are nearly pure-blood Indians, with many who have a mixture of Spanish, and a few of partially African stock. Those of mixed race are most numerous at Moyogalpa, where they have come from the mainland in comparatively late years. In physique the Indians are usually rather short, low-browed, with dark copper skin and thick coarse hair. On and near Madera are a few of commanding stature, many of the men being over six feet high, and the women proportionately large. The head is short, the features strongly marked, with heavy lower jaw and large teeth. I am inclined to believe that these are a remnant of an older tribe inhabiting the island. There are traditions pointing that way, and these people are more reticent and suspicious than the others, seeming still to have reverence for their ancient gods, and showing no disposition to guide me to the idols. As recently as 1850 Mr. Squier found many words of the Aztec language spoken by the Indians of Ometepec.

The absence of springs and streams confines the population to the shore of the lake, the latter supplying excellent drinking water and fish in abundance.

URN BURIAL.

Almost everywhere in the cultivated belt south of Moyogalpa may be found relics of the ancient inhabitants, and in the woods that clothe the foot hills are still to be seen the gods of their idolatry. About half a mile south of the village, the hacienda of Don José Angel Luna was placed at my disposition during the months of February, March, and April, 1876, with free permission to dig wherever I chose. (For plan see page 8.)

The first work was done in the northern boundary ditch of the estate, at a point about a hundred yards from the house and eighty from the lake. For convenience of reference this was called *Campo Santo*, the burial ground. Here were obtained twenty-eight burial urns, besides smaller vessels in terra cotta, beads, shells, &c.

The accompanying section shows the geological formation down into a stratum of black sand. The sand was quite thick at this point, and the excavation did not go through it; but in other places a hard, gritty ash was found underlying.

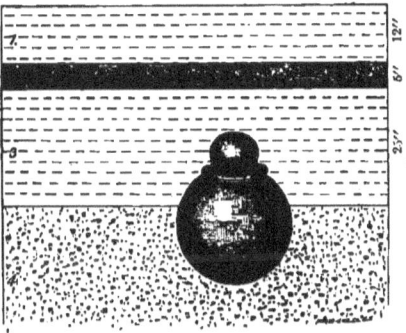

Section showing position of burial urn, Campo Santo.

No. 1 of the section was of light ash and volcanic cinder, with rich soil on top. The cinder predominated towards the bottom.

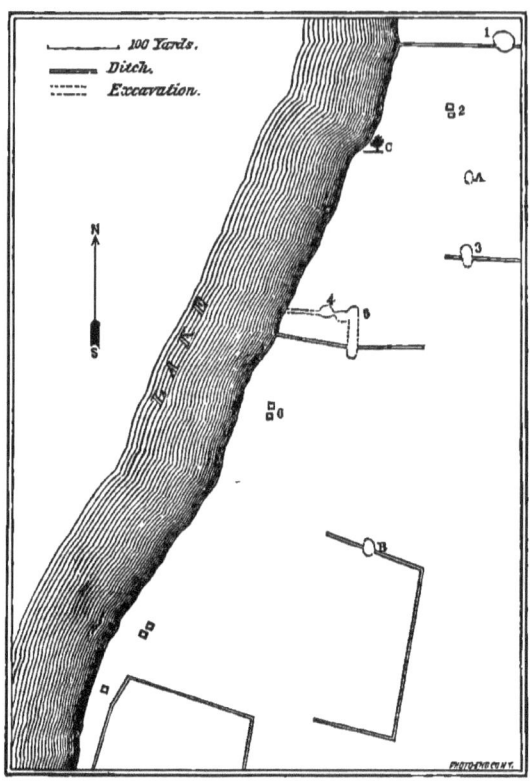

PLAN OF EXCAVATIONS AT LUNA'S.

A. Shards under lava. B. Jars in ditch. C. Aguacato tree. 1. Campo Santo. 2. Luna's house.
3. Pueblo Viejo. 4. Lopez Mine. 5. La Dominga. 6. House of Mercedes Cruz.

No. 2 was a layer of old lava, much decomposed, looking like a cake of cinder.

No. 3, of gritty ash, much like the main body of No. 1.

No. 4 was of black sand similar to that now forming the neighboring beach.

The first urn exhumed was spherical in form, with a round pot-shaped cap. The urn was 26 inches in diameter and $\frac{7}{16}$ inch in thickness. The diameter of the cap was 18 inches, with a depth of 13. One of the workmen, five feet five inches high and weighing 125 pounds, squatted comfortably in this urn, his head

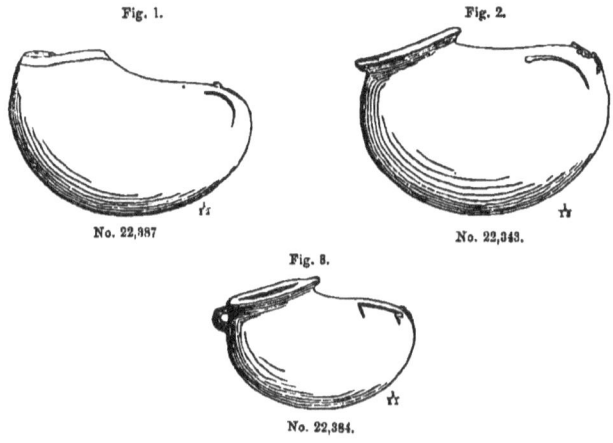

Oblong burial urns.

being amply covered by the cap. The urn was ornamented with raised serpentine tracings.

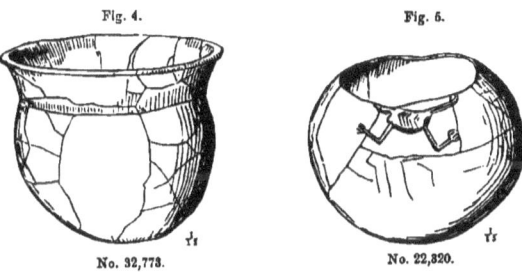

Round burial urns.

On the end of No. IV*, an oblong urn, was the representation of a human face in bold relief. Grotesque faces were of frequent occurrence on the pottery, and, in some cases, were strikingly expressive of broad humor.

In No. V, a femur was nearly perpendicular, the lower end up, as in sitting on the haunches with the knees drawn up to the chin. In many urns the bones of the thigh and leg were found in the flexed position of the knee, indicating the above posture. There was very little earth in No. V. On each side, in place of a handle, was a raised representation of a monkey.

The rim of No. VIII had been broken off to make the cap fit. This was found to be the case in many instances; and, with the great variety in the size and shape of the urns, was strongly suggestive of the idea that these vessels were made for general use, and not intended especially for burial purposes.

On the end of No. IX was a good representation, in relief, of a snake of venomous appearance.

These urns were usually found at a depth of about three feet, although some were four and a half, while in one case the top of the cap was only twenty inches from the surface. The bones were very soft and friable. The skull was usually in the centre, with the other bones around, as if fallen from a squatting position. Very little earth was in the well-closed jars, the others were filled.

Fig. 6.

No. 23,400.

Cap of small oblong burial urn.

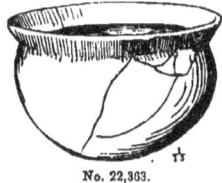

Fig. 7.

No. 22,363.

Cap of round burial urn.

No. XIV was notable for a double cap, and the end of No. XVI for the figure of an alligator, executed with much spirit.

The skull in No. XVII was perfect, but fell apart on exposure. It was lying on the side of the head and face, the right temple down. The irregular positions in which the skulls were found indicate that the skeletons were buried intact, and fell apart as the attachments gave way. The skull in XIX was lying on the vertex, with the occiput to the south.

No. XXI, jar and cap, had a broad flaring rim.

In the southern boundary line of the hacienda the ditch for a cactus hedge exposed burial urns similar to those at Campo Santo. This mine, called La

---

* The Roman numbers refer to the order in which the urns were exhumed.

ARCHÆOLOGICAL RESEARCHES IN NICARAGUA. 11

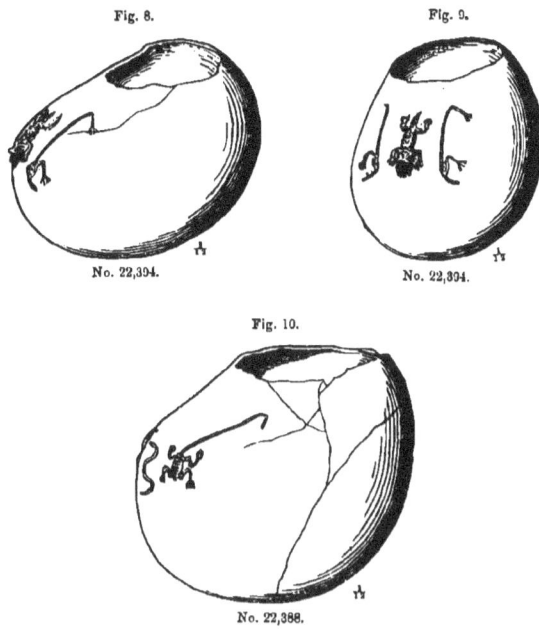

Oblong burial urns.

Dominga, was about four hundred yards, a little west of south, from the house, and ninety from the lake. The lava here was nearer the surface, the surface itself being lower than at Campo Santo. There was no ash of consequence immediately over the black sand, which was here underlying the lava. Under the sand was the usual hard ash. The continuous excavation was about twenty-five yards long, fifteen or twenty feet wide, and three or four feet deep, with a ditch offset towards the lake at each end. The lava in some cases seemed to have run and hardened around the urns, though this was not sufficiently well defined to be positively asserted. One jar had some underneath. If, as is probable, the burials were in the lake beach, the sand may have been washed from around it prior to the eruption, or in the violent agitations which accompanied it. Many of the urns, which were damp and soft when first exposed, had been broken by the roots of trees growing through the cracks. The cinder was looser and less well defined immediately above the jars. I believe it hardly possible that it was cut through for the interments, but that to the greater activity in chemical change above the urns and the growth of roots, encouraged by the richer soil, is due the loose condition of the cinder layer. There was no regular arrangement of the urns; which seemed to follow an old irregular beach, with general direction north and south, in a line about ten feet across. The jars were grouped, almost touching in some places. Those from XXV to CLVIII inclusive, with the exception of No. CXXX, were from La Dominga.

The bones in No. XXVIII were blackened by fire, and among those in No. XXIX was a piece of burnt bone. The latter jar was one of the largest, being 29 inches in diameter, 22 inches deep, and 15 across the mouth. The top was only ten inches below the surface.

Fig. 11.

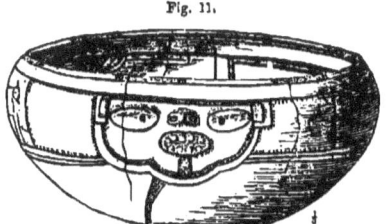

No. 22,866.
Cap of urn XXXV (outside.)

Fig. 12.

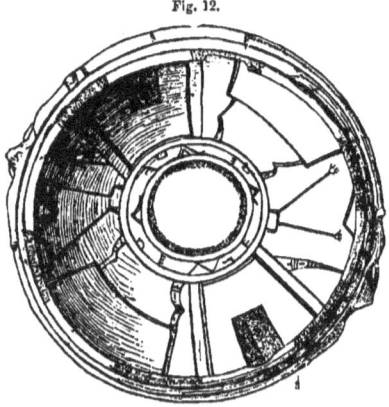

No. 22,866.
Cap of urn XXXV (inside.)

An ornament, in the position of a handle, on No. XXXIII was a laughing face. The ornaments on these large jars were always in relief, luted on, and not strong enough for service as handles.

No. XXXV, an oblong jar, was lying on its side. The fancifully painted cap was in position, and closed it so completely that but little earth had entered. Just beside it were two fancy bowls blackened by fire.

No. XXXIX had two caps, a fancy bowl, and one shaped like a pot, with a flat bottom. Near by were several painted plates and bowls and a water jar. In one place the smaller jars were piled on each other, and several times bones were found outside the jars.

No. XLVI had a simple slit in one side, and star-shaped holes in the other three. Possibly it was set in shallow water, and used to preserve fish alive.

The cap to No. LX, Fig. 4, was too small, and had slipped in.

The small urns, which were used for children, were more apt to contain beads and other ornaments. Marine shells were found in many jars, usually with holes for strings.

Fig. 13.

No. 22,371.

Painted bowl found outside urn No. LXVII.

Fig. 14.

No. 22,811.

Painted bowl, cap of urn No. LXIX.

Fig. 15.

No. 22,357.

Painted plate.

There was great variety in the shape and quality of the caps. The spherical jars generally had earthenware, pot-shaped caps, of material similar to that of the jars, while the oblong jars, as a rule, had painted fancy caps of various shapes, the shallow bowl-form predominating. These seemed to have been intended for household purposes, and were used here in emergencies, or when affection prompted extravagance.

The rim of No. LXXXII was forty-four inches below the surface.

No. LXXXIX contained 38 teeth, two left temporal and two occipital bones. Most of the bones were too much decayed to be recognized.

The spherical and oblong jars had no definite relative arrangement. The spherical jars and caps frequently had flaring pedestals, which were neither ornamental nor useful for burial purposes, another indication that they were not primarily or solely intended for this purpose.

In No. XCIII the cranium was on the earth near the rim, the lower jaw at the bottom of the jar, and the long bones nearly vertical in position. The attachments of the lower jaw probably gave way before the dirt got in.

The bones in these urns were so soft, and crumbled so readily on exposure to the air, that my offer of a reward for a good skull only secured one, although nearly two hundred skeletons—or portions rather—were disinterred.

Fig. 16.
No. 22,360.
Deep bowl, painted.

Fig. 17. 
No. 22,310.
Painted vase.

No. CXXVIII contained small bones and black beads.

In No. CXLII, a round jar, the skull was lying against the rim of the jar, which had early been filled with the earth sifting in between jar and cap.

Just in and under the burnt crust, which was not very well defined here, was jar No. CLVIII, with cap in position near the surface. The bones were more than usually well preserved. They had been kept in place by the earth filling the jar early. The skull was upright. The atlas had not been disarticulated, nor had any of the other vertebræ; the spine being in position as sitting in the bottom of the urn, with the knees in the toe end (shoe-shaped or oblong jar) and the feet underneath. The large jars were buried deep enough in the hard ground to bring their tops on a level with those of smaller ones in the sand.

In the ditch between the northern end of the excavation and the lake, at the point marked Lopez mine, the sand had disappeared, and in the hard earth underlying the lava were slab-stones, apparently worn by use, standing around as if in a habitation, and fragments of pottery, similar to that afterwards found in abundance at Santa Helena, with a stone dish and human bones. The dish of basalt was immediately under lava ten inches thick. There was one large flattened jar of strange shape, No. CXXX. It was about twenty-five inches in diameter, and contained only teeth and dirt. These relics belong to an entirely distinct class, and will be described further on.

Burial urns were exposed in the ditch at B, on a southern projection of the line of excavation, and were reported to have been found at the aguacate tree, near where a prolongation of the line north strikes the beach.

The plan on page 8 is given merely to facilitate description. The bearings were by pocket compass, and distances, when taken, were paced. The ditches shown averaged 2½ feet deep. The lava was found everywhere at about the same depth, in wavy lines, as if to fit inequalities of the surface. In several places under it were found collections of cobble-like lava stones. These may have been collected to clear the land for cultivation. In other portions of the island they are strewn over the surface, and in many places the beach is lined with the same stones worn round.

Below is a condensed tabulated statement of the urns, in the order in which they were disinterred, the first column containing the number of the jar and its shape; the second, the shape and material of the cap, using the word *earthen* where the material was the same as that of the ordinary jar, and the word *painted*[*] where of finer manufacture, painted bowls, &c. Under the head *position* is the point of the compass towards which the skeleton faced, or to which the toe end of the shoe-shaped jar pointed. In the column for size the abbreviation *dia.* signifies diameter, *dep.* depth, *th.* thickness, *l.* length, *cir.* circumference, *br.* breadth, *j.* jar, and *c.* cap. The figures in this column refer to inches.

DETAILED LIST OF URNS EXHUMED.

Jar.	Cap.	Size.	Position.	Contents.
I Round	1	j. {dia. 20, th. ⅞, dia. 1⅞} c. {dep. 13}		Adult human bones.
II Oblong. III "	1	j. {l. 19, cir. 36, mouth 7}		Small bones and earthen dish.
IV "	"	j. {l. 28, br. 19, dep. 22, th. ½, dia. 1⅞} c. {dep. 13}		Adult bones and teeth, two marine shells with holes for string.
V Round	"			Large bones and black beads.
VI "	"			Bones, small piece of stone.
VII "		j. dia. 16		Bones, black and small shell-beads.
VIII Oblong	1	j. {l. 25, br. 15, dep. 15, th. ½} c. {br. 12, dep. 9}		Bones, green stone beads.

* These painted cups were of the class styled Luna terra-cotta.

ARCHÆOLOGICAL RESEARCHES IN NICARAGUA.

DETAILED LIST OF URNS EXHUMED—Continued.

Jar.		Cap.	Size.	Position.	Contents.
IX	Oblong	1	j. { l. 23 / cir. 57 / th. ½ }		Whitish beads, bones.
X	"	"			Bones.
XI	Round	"			Bones, adult, thick skull.
XII	"	"			Bones, small black beads.
XIII	Oblong	"			Bones, shell ornament, with hole for string.
XIV	Round	2	{ ½. dia. 18 / Inner c. dia. 12 }		Bones and teeth, green beads.
XV	Oblong	1		S.	Bones, black beads.
XVI	"	"		S.	" "
XVII	"	"	j. { l. 29½ / br. 22¼ / dep. 23 }	S.	Bones, white shell beads, one black bead, small object in black pottery.
XVIII	Oblong	"		S.	Bones.
XIX	Round		j. { dia. 15 / dep. 13 }		"
XX	"	1	c. { dia. 22 / dep. 15 }		" Jar and cup about same size.
XXI	"	"	j. { dia. 19 / dep. 16 } c. { dia. 17½ / dep. 18 }		Bones.
XXII	"	"	j. { dia. 25 / dep. 10 / mouth, 9½ } c. { dia. 13½ / dep. 0 }		"
XXIII	"	"			Bones and long black beads.
XXIV	"	"			Bones.
XXV	Oblong	"			Bones, lava stones, and a small jar.
XXVI	"	"			Bones.
XXVII	"			S.	
XXVIII	"	1		S.	A few blackened bones.
XXIX	Round		j. { dia. 20 / dep. 22 / mouth, 15 }		Piece burnt bone, painted plate.
XXX	Oblong				A few small young bones.
XXXI	"		Small	S.	Small jur near.
XXXII	"		"		Piece of charcoal.
XXXIII	"	1, painted	Medium	S.	Flint chip.
XXXIV	"	"			Bones, plate, and stone pestle.
XXXV	"	" painted			Two fancy bowls near, blackened by heat.
XXXVI	"	1, painted		N. W.	
XXXVII	"	2 "		S. W.	
XXXVIII	Round	1			Bones, skull very thick.
XXXIX	"	2, painted	j. dia. 20		Bones, long red beads.
XL	Oblong		Small	S. E.	A few white shell beads.
XLI	"				Bones in earth near by.
XLII	"				Bones and a few black beads.
XLIII	"				
XLIV	"				
XLV	Round	1	j. dia. 18		Temporal bone of child, crowns of two teeth, little painted jar, bowl, painted plate, small oblong vessel, and small white bead.
XLVI	"				
XLVII	Oblong		Small		A few small bones, two gold beads strongly alloyed with copper, white beads.
XLVIII	"	1	"		
XLIX	Round	"	j. { dia. 28 / dep. 20 }		Bones.
L	"				Bones, large.
LI	Oblong				
LII	"	1	Rather large	W.	White beads, bones near by.
LIII	Round	"	Medium		Crowns of molars unworn, white and red beads.

ARCHÆOLOGICAL RESEARCHES IN NICARAGUA.

DETAILED LIST OF URNS EXHUMED—Continued.

Jar.		Cap.	Size.	Position.	Contents.
LIV	Oblong	1	Medium	S. W.	Thin bones, crowns of young teeth, painted flask and bowl, marine shells, 18 black beads, piece of pretty stone, black vessel shaped like young duck, a painted cup on the cap.
LV	"	"		N. E.	Crowns of teeth.
LVI	"			S. W.	
LVII	"			S.	" "
LVIII	"				" "
LIX	"				A few bones.
LX	Round	1	j. {dia. 20, dep. 18}		Bones.
LXI	Oblong	" earthen			Bones, thin
LXII	"	" painted.			
LXIII	"	"			
LXIV	"	" earthen.			
LXV	"	" "		S.	Thin cranial bones, unworn crowns of teeth, black beads, piece of pretty stone, black vessel shaped like young duck, a painted cup on the cap.
LXVI	"	1, painted plate			Bones, a green and a black bead.
LXVII	Round	" earthen	j. {dia. 20, dep. 18½, mouth. 8} c. {dia. 12, dep. 12}		Brown beads, bones.
LXVIII	Oblong	" "	c. dia. 10	S. E.	Young bones, black beads, spindle whorl outside.
LXIX	"	" painted bowl.	Small		Young bones.
LXX	"	" earthen	c. {dia. 11, dep. 8}		
LXXI	"	" "	Quite large	W.	Bones.
LXXII	"	" "	l. 16		Bones, young
LXXIII	"	1, painted vase.			
LXXIV	"	" earthen	Medium	S. E.	Small piece of jadeite like a watch seal, with hole for string, green, black,and red beads,cup and plates.
LXXV	"	" "	Small		Crowns of teeth and black beads.
LXXVI	"	" "			Teeth, small black cup, bones of small animal.
LXXVII	"	" "			Bones.
LXXVIII	Round	"			Bones and black beads.
LXXIX	Oblong	"	Small		Portion of temporal bone.
LXXX	Round	" earthen	j. dia. 20, c. {dia. 20, dep. 11}		Adult bones.
LXXXI	Oblong			W.	Crowns of teeth, grain of burnt corn.
LXXXII	Round	1, bell-shaped			Beads.
LXXXIII	Oblong	" earthen	j. Medium. c. {dia. 10½, dep. 8}		Young bones.
LXXXIV	"		Medium	S. W.	Bones and teeth.
LXXXV	"	1, painted bowl			" "
LXXXVI	"	" black pot	Rather small		Thin cranial bones and teeth.
LXXXVII	Round		j. {dia. 21, dep. 10}		
LXXXVIII	"	1, earthen	j. {dia. 17, dep. 13} c. {dia. 15, dep. 11}		
LXXXIX	"	" "	j. {dia. 23½, dep. 17½} c. {dia. 18, dep. 15}		2 left temporal bones, 2 occipital, and 38 teeth. Many bones too decayed to be recognized.
XC	"	"			Adult bones.
XCI	Oblong	" earthen			Teeth, beans.
XCII	Round	" "	j. dia. 20		Bones.
XCIII	"	" "	j. {dia. 15½, dep. 12½} c. {dia. 14, dep. 11}		Bones.

ARCHÆOLOGICAL RESEARCHES IN NICARAGUA.

DETAILED LIST OF URNS EXHUMED—Continued.

Jar.		Cap.	Size.	Position.	Contents.
XCIV	Round	1.			
XCV	"	" earthen	j. dia. 20 / c. dia. 15½		Human bones, and bones of a small animal.
XCVI	Oblong	" "		W.	
XCVII	"	" "			Teeth.
XCVIII	"	" "		S. E.	
XCIX	"	" "	Small		Young bones, and representation of frog in shell.
C	"	" "	Medium		Small bones, black beads, something like a grain of coffee.
CI	Round	"	"		Bones, large cranium—broad, and rather flat on top.
CII	Oblong	" earthen			Bones.
CIII	"	" painted			Black cup.
CIV	"	" vase.			
CV	"	" earthen	Medium		Bones.
CVI	Round	" "	About 20, j. and c.		
CVII	Oblong	" painted bowl			Bones, small, black beads and a green one.
CVIII	Round	" earthen	j. { dia. 10 / dep. 19 }		White beads and shells. (Cap about size of jar.)
CIX	"	"	j. { dia. 18 / dep. 12 } c. { dia. 16 / dep. 14½ }		Adult bones, green beads, and whistle.
CX	"	" earthen bowl	j. { dia. 17 / dep. 14 } c. { dia. 17 / dep. 13 }		Black beads.
CXI	"	" bowl	j. { dia. 22½ / dep. 15 } c. { dia. 20½ / dep. 14 }		Bones, two adult crania.
CXII	Oblong	" earthen	Small		Bones.
CXIII	Round	" "	j. { dia. 15 / dep. 12 } c. { dia. 13 / dep. 8 }		Bones, cranium of young person.
CXIV	"	"			Saucer.
CXV	Oblong				Bones.
CXVI	Round	" painted bowl			Thin cranial bones.
CXVII	Oblong				Small bones and black beads.
CXVIII	"	1, earthen			Small vase.
CXIX	"				Bones and teeth.
CXX	Round				Bones.
CXXI	"				"
CXXII	"				"
CXXIII	"				"
CXXIV	Oblong				"
CXXV	"				"
CXXVI	"				Green bead.
CXXVII	Round	1.	j. { dia. 19 / dep. 15 } c. { dia. 18 / dep. 16 }		Bones.
CXXVIII	Painted		Small		Small bones and black beads.
CXXIX	Round	1.	About 20 in dia.		Green and gold beads.
CXXX	Flat	1, flat	About 25 in dia.		Teeth.
CXXXI	Oblong				Bones.
CXXXII	"	1, earthen			Bones and green beads.
CXXXIII	"	" "	Small		Bones, black beads, small water jar.
CXXXIV	Round	"			Bones, green beads, gold image, and marine shells.
CXXXV	Oblong	" earthen	Small.		
CXXXVI	"			W.	Bones and long black beads.
CXXXVII	"				Teeth and black beads.
CXXXVIII	"				Bones.
CXXXIX	Round				"
CXL	"				Bones and large black beads.

DETAILED LIST OF URNS EXHUMED—Continued.

Jar.	Cap.	Size.	Position.	Contents.
CXLI Round	1			Bones and small green beads, piece of stone roller under the jar.
CXLII "	"	j. { dia. 19½ / dep. 13 } c. { dia. 17 / dep. 11 }		Bones.
CXLIII "				"
CXLIV Oblong				"
CXLV Round		j. dia. 20		Bones and white beads, celt near.
CXLVI "	"	j. about 17 dia.		
CXLVII "	"	j. about 17 dia.		Black beads.
CXLVIII Oblong.				
CXLIX "	" earthen		N. W.	Green beads.
CL Round	" painted bowl			Bones, green and black beads, beans.
CLI Oblong	" earthen			Seeds and marine shells.
CLII Round	" "	j. dia. 23		Bones. (Small mouth.)
CLIII Oblong	" "	Medium.		
CLIV "	" "			Pretty cups and plates, painted and black.
CLV "	" painted	Small		Small bones, no teeth.
CLVI "	" earthen	Medium	S. W.	Bones, young teeth, green beads, and marine shells.
CLVII Round		"		Bones and black beads.
CLVIII Oblong	1			Bones.
CLIX Round	"	Small		Small bones.
CLX Oblong		Medium.		
CLXI Round	1	j. { dia. 20 / dep. 17 } c. { dia. 18 / dep. 18 }		Adult bones.
CLXII "	" painted	Large		Two fancy black cups, sea shells for necklace. (Small mouth to jar.)

RECAPITULATION.

Jar.	No. Examined.	No. with Caps.	No. containing		Position.					
			Human Bones.	Beads.	S.	W.	N.W.	N. E.	S.W.	S. E.
Oblong	96	61	63	27	10	5	2	1	5	4
Round	66	53	55	25						
Total	162	114	118	52						

The first twenty-four and last four jars were from Campo Santo. The others were from La Dominga, except No. CXXX, from the Lopez mine.

Bones of young children originally in some of the small jars may have entirely disappeared, thus lessening the proportion of those containing osseous remains.

LUNA TERRA-COTTA.

Often serving as caps for the burial urns, or within or near them, were found the small painted vessels frequently alluded to before. Their extraordinary style of ornamentation marked them as a class with great distinctness. No fragment of this type was discovered, except in association with the burial urns. It was given the name of Luna ware, because it was first met with and found in greatest quantity on the hacienda of Don José Luna.

In the collection delivered to the Smithsonian Institution were thirty-eight pieces of this terra-cotta—six of which were afterwards sent to the Peabody Museum of American Archæology and Ethnology at Harvard University. The Smithsonian has, in addition, seven specimens from the collection of Captain J. M. Dow, one presented by Commander E. P. Lull, U. S. N., and one of unknown origin. All of these will be used here, to make the illustration and description more complete. Credit is given by mention of the Smithsonian numbers. Captain Dow's are Nos. 299, 300, 301, 304, 309, 310, and 313; Commander Lull's is 14,104, and the unknown, 7,509. In the whole collection of forty-seven specimens there are thirty-three bowls and two fragments; eight vases, of which two are tripods; three plates; one cup; and an image of a man.

The Luna terra-cotta was not thoroughly burned, and on exposure, after having laid for centuries in the damp alluvium, it was moist, and had to be handled with care. Exposure to the air, in the shade at first and then in the sun, soon hardened it. The body was of clay, mixed with sand.

No evidence of the use of shells appeared; but as limestone abounds in other districts of the department of Rivas, it is highly probable that chemical analysis would show the presence of lime. The biscuit is of a reddish brown, and seems to have been more thoroughly baked in some pieces than others. A thick coat of cream or buff paint was laid on, and the designs painted in brown, occasionally in red, the brown line sometimes having a red one on one side. There is no glaze on this pottery. The surface was probably smoothed and polished, as is now done in the same neighborhood, by rubbing the wet surface with a smooth stick or stone. The paint was afterwards laid on, and heat apparently again applied. There is not a piece showing the effects of a temperature sufficiently high to have vitrified a glaze. The style of the painted designs is entirely distinct from that of any other pottery that I have seen, and would not be mistaken or confounded with other prehistoric American ware by the most careless observer. The designs are conventional and awkward, but remarkably distinctive. No attempt at the representation of natural objects is seen, except a figure on the inside of certain bowls, which was possibly intended to represent a monkey; and on the outside of several others, in the position of two handles on opposite sides, are human faces or masks in relief, whose features have been more fully indicated by painted outlines. Similar faces are on the outside of the legs of a tripod in the Dow collection, and the feet of the tripod, No. 14,104, are grotesque heads, probably caricatures of the human head.

The vessels commonly have on the outside a band of lines around near the rim, and another about half way down. The intervening space is divided into panels* occupied by conventional designs, not symmetrical, but drawn from left to right, and following as in profile. In the general character of the coloring and the Luna patterns there is a resemblance to the Marajo pottery of Brazil, collected and described by Prof. Hartt; but the drawing on the latter is in much more regular geometrical style, and incised ornaments are of frequent occurrence, while they are never seen on the Luna ware.

It is rather a singular fact that this terra-cotta was associated in and around the burial urns with black earthen ware, which was ornamented with faces in relief and incised borders in fret, &c. Again, the absence of the *relievo* representations of animals, especially reptiles, which adorned the burial urns, indicates a difference in the fashion for different kinds of vessels. The work with the brush on the Luna terra-cotta is singularly cramped, while decided spirit is shown in the figures on the large urns. It almost looks as if different people had manufactured the two varieties, and that to commerce or conquest was due the interchange of articles. On nearly all these bowls, and on many of the urns, the surface is traced over in delicate irregularly arborescent or veined lines of bluish black, which add decidedly to the beauty of the ware. These lines were rather puzzling at first, but seem to be the result of the burning into charcoal of fine rootlets, which interlaced the clay. The color was brought out in burning, so as to show through the paint. The extension of these lines for considerable distances in some of the specimens indicates that the smaller vessels were moulded by hand, and not built up by the rope method. They were much rarer and shorter in the large vessels.

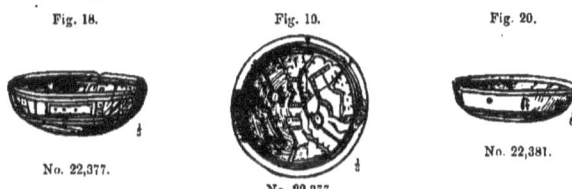

Fig. 18.   Fig. 19.   Fig. 20.

No. 22,377.   No. 22,377.   No. 22,381.

Shallow bowls of Luna terra-cotta.

Of the individual specimens the little shallow bowl or dish, No. 22,377, Figs.

---

* Not used in the strict architectural sense of the term.

18, 19, is the smallest in size and simplest in form, but is painted in intricate design, especially within. The want of mathematical precision in the form of this and the rather larger bowl, Fig. 20, shows at once the absence of the potter's wheel in their manufacture. The particular marks on these pieces will be noticed later.

Fig. 21.

No. 22,365.—Bowl of Luna terra-cotta.

In Fig. 21 is seen a bowl of the average shape, but in ornamentation rather peculiar, the red predominating in broad bands and surfaces in the upper half of the outside, leaving the figures in buff. The cross occurs three times between panels which have no counterpart in the collection. The buff of the inner surface is relieved only by a black line at the rim, with a red one a little lower. On the outside just below the panel work is a narrow band, then two more a little lower still. In the interval a succession of figures in fret surround the bowl. This ornament is found on fourteen specimens. The lower line of the band of

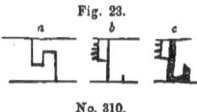

Fig. 22.

No. 22,314.

frets is touched by the limbs of the cross, (Fig. 22,) which, with slight variations in detail, occurs on all but four of the bowls. The modifications were usually in the ornamentation of the ends of the limbs, as in a, b, and c. The bowls which fail to have this cross, have the plain buff field on the outside, with only a line or band of lines around the edge, their peculiar designs being within. One of these is shown in Figs. 11 and 12.

The fret mentioned above is the subject of infinite variation; even on the same vessel no two forms are exactly alike. Indeed, in ornamenting this terra-cotta the painter seems to have had certain conventional designs in his mind, which he executed without rigid accuracy in detail.

Fig. 23.

No. 310.

In *a*, Fig. 23, is illustrated the simplest form of the fret used. In No. 310 there is a band above and below the main panels inside and out. In that on the outer margin of the rim, *a* alternates with *c*, while in the other three bands it alternates with *b*. The number of points on the upper left hand side of *c* varies from two to four, always facing the same way, not right and left, as in the foot-

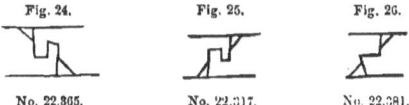

prints of the Aztec picture-writings. Fig. 24 presents the common form, drawn from left to right. This is reversed in Figs. 25 and 26, the only exceptions. In Fig. 27 there is a combination of a scallop and a form even simpler than *a* in Fig. 23; and Fig. 28 shows, in *a*, a slight modification of *b*, Fig. 23 occupying the

space left after the introduction of five of the figures *b*. The figures resembling foot-prints occur on seventeen and the fret on fourteen pieces. Instead of the development of the simplest and purest form into the meander, current fret, and other graceful patterns discussed by Prof. Hartt,* these painters dropped into awkward conventional expressions of the greatest variety and irregularity in detail. The illustrations show the utter impossibility of a clear written description of these figures. They occur on sixteen specimens of the collection, and range from that in Fig. 29, which is very slightly different from *c*, Fig. 23, up to the remarkable forms in Figs. 34 and 35.

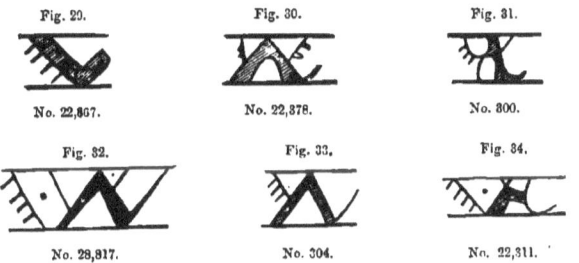

---

* Evolution in Ornament: C. F. Hartt in Popular Science Monthly, January, 1875.

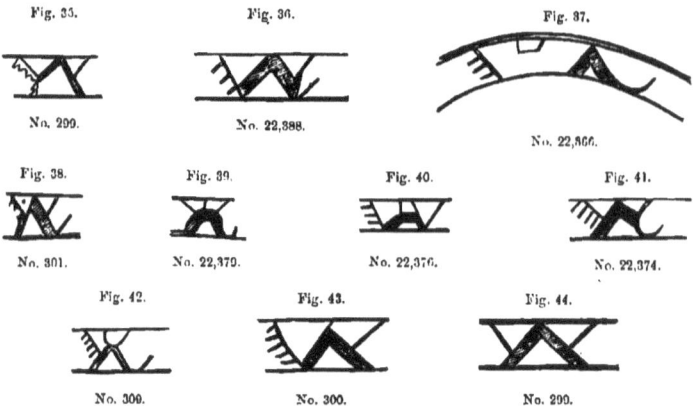

In No. 22,356, Fig. 45, we have the simplest form of the shallow bowl modified by the introduction of new designs, and the presence of faces in relief. Midway between the faces is seen a narrow panel with a zigzag ornament, on each

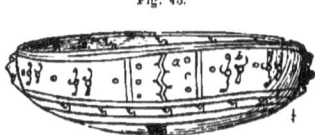

No. 22,356.—Bowl of Luna terra-cotta.

side of which is a line of small rings or circles. On the inner surface this figure is found, nearly behind the faces, the intervening panels having the peculiar figure *b* repeated three times on each side. The zigzag is found on eight pieces. As elsewhere, no rigid adherence to pattern is observed; but irregularities, apparently the result of carelessness, mark the execution. This is shown in Fig. 46, where the angles are only two on a side, while there are eight circles. Between two of the three lines of the zigzag the decoration is enriched by horizontal black lines and red surfaces. In No. 22,317, from which the illustration was taken, this occurs on opposite sides, painted in the same direction; that is, with extra coloring between the middle and right line. In Figs. 47 and 48 the shading is in opposite directions on the same bowls. On each of these two specimens the figure is found twice on the outside. In No. 22,381 it occurs twice on the inside, and in 22,388 three times within and twice outside. The circles in these panels

ARCHÆOLOGICAL RESEARCHES IN NICARAGUA. 25

Fig. 46.

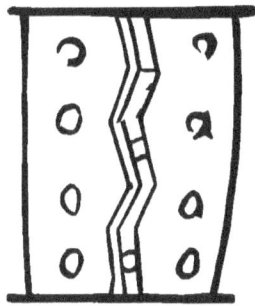

No. 22,317.

Fig. 47.

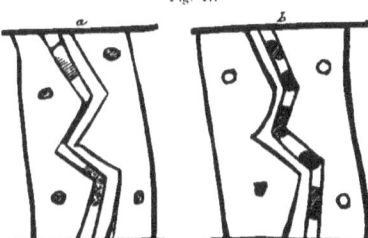

No. 22,311.

Fig. 48.

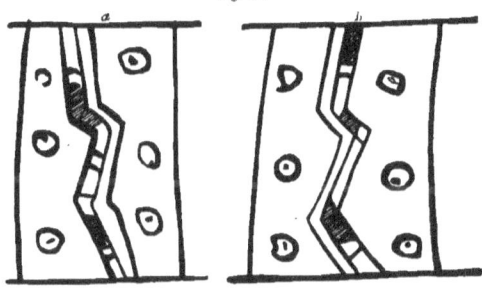

No. 22,316.

4

occasionally have dots in the centre, which seem to have been daubed in wherever the painter thought that more color was desirable.

The figures at *b*, Fig. 45, are probably the most curious found on this pottery, and have more the appearance of hieroglyphs. But the regularity of their arrangement and their frequent and symmetrical repetition on the same vessel, indicate that they were used here as ornaments. They may have been taken from the hieroglyphic system of another people, and adopted as ornamental in the same way that single letters of our alphabet are now often seen on stoneware. This figure occurs in ten specimens. In No. 22,356, Fig. 45, the black boundary lines of the panel *b* are shaded with red, and so are the central figures. In addition to those in the panels inside and out, the peculiar forms occur also in the bottom of the bowl, as shown at *c*, Fig. 45. These forms are found in nine pieces of the collection. Among the best examples are those to be seen on No.

Fig. 49.

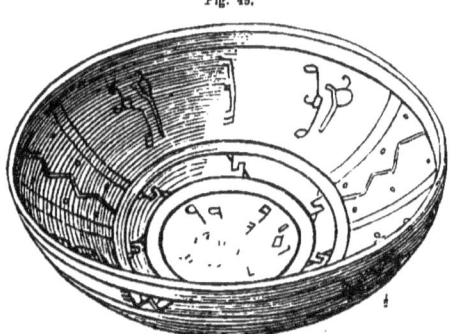

No. 28,817.—Inside of bowl of Luna terra-cotta.

28,817, a pretty bowl from Chilaite. In the bottom of this specimen the four pairs are arranged with feet in the centre in a sort of rosette. On the inside of the vessel is a band around the bottom, in which the simpler fret occurs seven times, while outside the conventional modification of the same is seen repeated

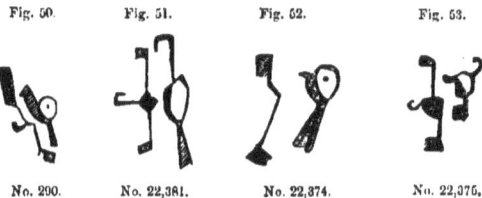

Fig. 50.   Fig. 51.   Fig. 52.   Fig. 53.

No. 290.   No. 22,381.   No. 22,374.   No. 22,375.

five times. The series of illustrations of the hieroglyph-like figures shows some of the variations in detail indulged in by the artist.

In No. 299, a bowl, with the faces in relief, Fig. 50, is repeated three times with the crucial form at *a* between. On the inside of No. 22,381 is Fig. 51 three times reproduced, with a circle separating the groups, while on 22,374 the awkward figure, Fig. 52, is seen on the outside twice on one side with a circle between, and once on the other. Fig. 53 on the outside of No. 22,375 occurs on each side three times with the usual circle intervening.

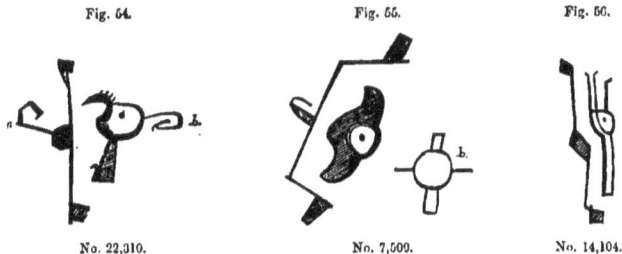

Fig. 54.   Fig. 55.   Fig. 56.

No. 22,310.   No. 7,509.   No. 14,104.

On No. 22,310 the figure, Fig. 54, is found four times on the outside, the fifth has been lost by the breaking out of a fragment. The circles shaded with red fill in the intervals. In this specimen the curls at *a* and *b* vary in direction. Fig. 55 is repeated four times around the inside of No. 7,509, alternating with *b*. It is produced once in the bottom. In each of the spaces between the feet of the tripod 14,104 is Fig. 56, with slight alterations.

These figures are probably conventional representations which vary so far from the original design as to be unrecognizable.

The design next to be considered is that noticed in Fig. 16, where panels of a novel variety may be observed. The study of this pattern shows what would have been a very interesting instance of evolution in ornament, if the specimens had only been discovered in different layers of geological formation or with surroundings indicating difference in age of deposit. But as they were nearly all from the same burial ground, and as the circumstances under which they were found gave no evidence of great difference in the dates of interment, the progressive arrangement of the series can only be used to show what may have been successive steps in development.

Fig. 57.   Fig. 58.

No. 22,377.   No. 22,354.

Fig. 57 is in the simplest style, although the outlines are clearer and more regular than usual. It occurs four times in a band just below the rim on the outside, on a field of dirty buff. The panel in Fig. 58 is repeated ten times with slight variations in No. 22,354. The form is slightly changed from the original by the separation of the two smaller squares from each other, and from the larger subdivision *a*, and by the right end of *a* being pointed and extended to partially fill in the new vacancy. This point is represented in Fig. 59 by three horizontal

Fig. 59. Fig. 60.
No. 22,371. No. 22,314.

lines, similar lines being found on the other end of the parallelogram. The color of this specimen, No. 22,371, is reddish yellow, and on it are six panels in which the number of dots differ. In Fig. 60 the surface in *a* is embellished by a perpendicular line in the centre with fine dots on each side. At first these dots were supposed to refer to dates or ages. But they vary in number in different panels of the same vessel in a manner to suggest that they were placed there without definite design, except to fill in and enrich the ornamentation. Thus, in No. 22,314 there are five panels, Fig. 60, of nearly the same dimensions, with the number of dots varying in the different lines, as follows:

	1st line.	2d line.	3d line.	4th line.	5th line.	Total.
1st panel,	13 +	6 +	5 +	5 +	7 =	36
2d panel,	11 +	7 +	6 +	6 +	6 =	36
3d panel,	11 +	8 +	7 +	6 +	6 =	38
4th panel,	9 +	7 +	6 +	6 +	6 =	34
5th panel,	12 +	8 +	5 +	4 +	6 =	35

The dots on most pieces were much more irregular in number than in this specimen. The field color is a yellowish cream, with dark brown lines bordered on one side of the upright lines with dirty yellow. In a great many pieces of this terra-cotta the bordering lines of red or yellow are laid on in the most careless manner, smearing over the black lines or leaving them entirely in some places. Another bowl is almost precisely similar in ornamentation to that last described.

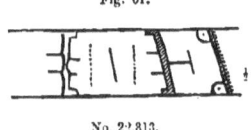

Fig. 61.
No. 22,813.

On No. 22,313 there are two complete panels and one incomplete (Fig. 61) on each side between the faces. The number of dots varies. It is a well-preserved specimen, and the lines show a regard for precision rarely seen in the collection.

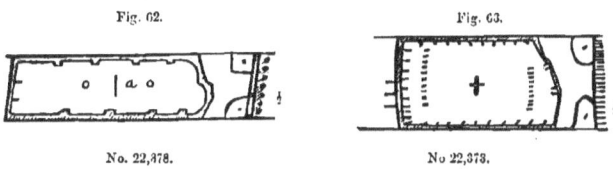

Fig. 62.   Fig. 63.

No. 22,378.   No 22,373.

In Fig. 62 will be observed a circle on each side of the perpendicular in *a*, and a crooked irregularity in the left-hand boundary line of the same figure. This panel occurs six times on No. 22,378. On No. 22,373 the panel is found four times, leaving a gap which was filled in apparently with the same pattern modified, the paint has been so much effaced as to leave the design uncertain. The panels on this specimen again differ from the last in having dashes in place of the circles, and the central perpendicular line crossed by a horizontal.

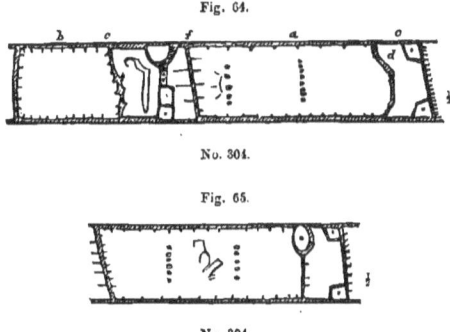

Fig. 64.

No. 304.

Fig. 65.

No. 304.

We are presented with the first step in radical change of this pattern in No. 304. Here the simple form in *a*, Fig. 64, is modified materially by a shaded line drawn between *c* and *d*, and the introduction in the vacant centre of *a*, of a figure, the remaining traces of which resemble to a certain extent the curious forms in Figs. 49–56. The paint just here has unfortunately been much worn. In the band around the bowl the panel, *a*, Fig. 64, was produced three times, and then that in Fig. 65; this was followed by two more of *a*, and the remaining space, too limited for Fig. 65, was filled in with *b*, Fig. 64. In this panel the whole of Fig. 65 seems to have been crowded into the space between *e* and *f*, the dots being omitted, the central form modified, and the two small squares on the right transferred to the lower left-hand corner of the same compartment. The carelessness and lack of foresight on the part of the painter—he could hardly be termed artist—is illustrated in the absence of a preconceived plan and measurements, while at the same time considerable ingenuity is shown, and power of accommodation to circumstances.

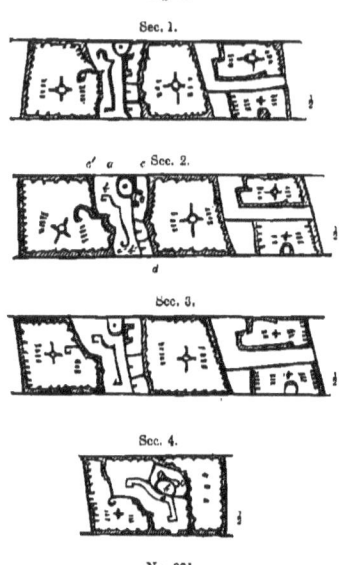

Fig. 66.

No. 301.

In 301 is seen another instance of this combination in form and adaptation to space. The sections form a band around the vessel. The principal pattern in sections 1, 2, and 3 is essentially similar to *b* in Fig. 64, with the variations in detail, which are so common. In the space remaining to complete the circumference was introduced the fourth section. In this the second section has been crowded and modified by drawing lines between *a* and *b*, *a'* and *b'*, lengthening the shaded line *c*, *d*, and bending the whole figure over to the left until *c* and *c'* met. The panel on the right of the first three sections was dropped entirely, and of the ornamentation in the field of the central one only three dashes were left.

ARCHÆOLOGICAL RESEARCHES IN NICARAGUA. 31

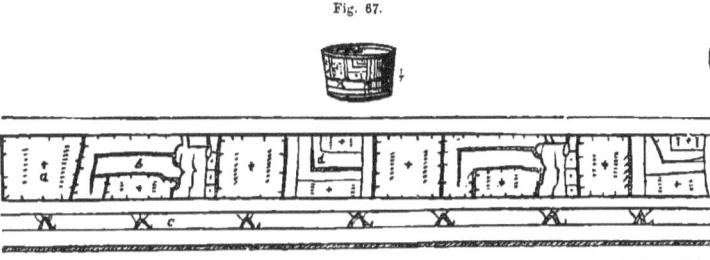

Fig. 67.

No. 22,379.

The whole of the outside ornamentation in the little cup No. 22,379 is illustrated in Fig. 67. At *b* is the same pattern as that considered in Fig. 66, alternating in this instance with the half pattern *d*, the simpler panel, *a*, intervening.

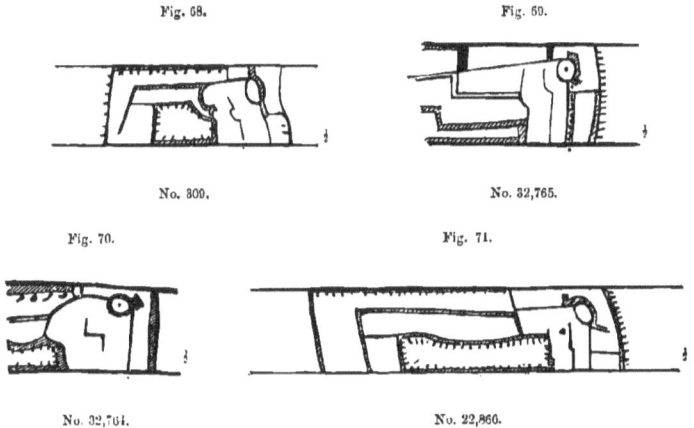

Fig. 68.   Fig. 69.

No. 309.   No. 32,765.

Fig. 70.   Fig. 71.

No. 32,764.   No. 22,860.

Here Figs. 68, 69, 70, 71 may be introduced as examples of successive steps in degeneration of the pattern into ruder representation. The figures 69 and 70 are on fragments of bowls.

A curious modification with distortion of this figure is shown in Fig. 72, where is seen the same design, almost exact in detail, inverted. In Fig. 73 it

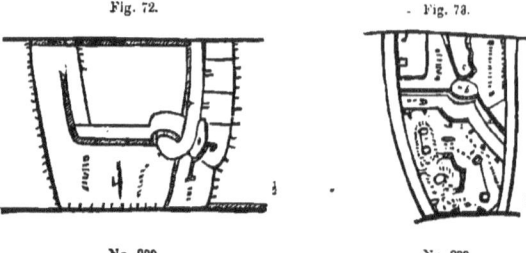

Fig. 72.   Fig. 73.

No. 299.   No. 299.

occurs again, in the crooked double lines at *a*, in which rests the circle or globe, and above the latter, the double lines with red and black shading, which were incipient at *c* in the fourth section of Fig. 66. The otherwise vacant spaces are filled in as usual with lines, circles, and dots, which vary in number and arrangement in the three panels.

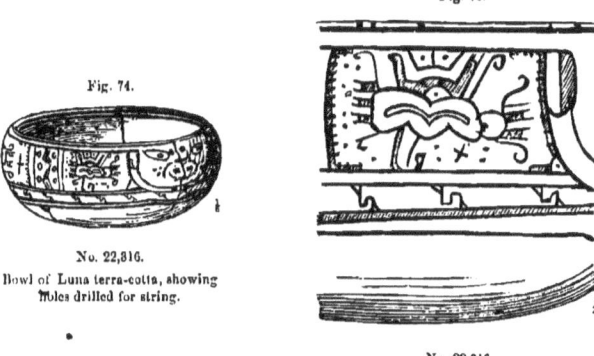

Fig. 74.

No. 22,316.
Bowl of Luna terra-cotta, showing holes drilled for string.

Fig. 75.

No. 22,316.

From this point we can pursue the trace of evolution into the series of more elaborate forms seen on No. 22,316, Figs. 74, 75, and six other specimens. The figure is found on the first four times, separated by the faces in relief and the zigzag panels alternately. The panel to the left of, and companion to that in the illustration, has a cross on each side of the figure, the arms of which are similar to those at *a* on the left side of Fig. 75, except that there is a horizontal black line above the red band or feather, and a circle where the cross is shown. The opposite panels are very like, first and third, second and fourth. The third has the arms inverted and a cross on the left. The fourth has a cross as in the first.

Fig. 76.

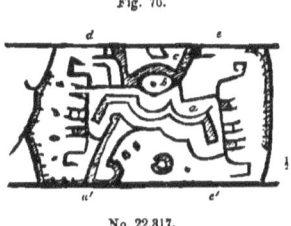

No. 22,317.

In Fig. 76 the similarity to section 4, Fig. 66, may be seen by placing sheets of paper on each side, cutting off the view of all but that portion of the figure between dd' and ee'. At a is the crook, b the circle, and c the plumes or wings. Below, the enclosed surface is enriched with dots and rings. Some

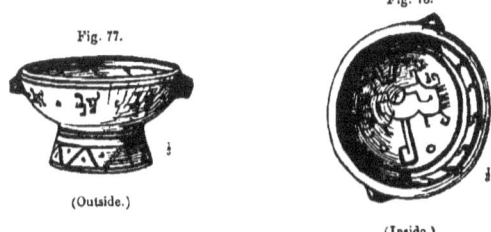

Fig. 77. (Outside.)   Fig. 78. (Inside.)

No. 22,375.—Vase of Luna terra-cotta.

Fig. 79.

No. 22,376.

resemblance, rather remote it is true, may be observed between the central figure and those illustrated in the series, Figs. 50–56. In the graceful little vase, No. 22,375, Figs. 77, 78, this pattern is painted in the bottom in quite elaborate style and with more regularity. The reliefs on this specimen are similar to the noses on the faces to be discussed later. This specimen in buff, with the lines in brown shaded with red, is the prettiest piece of the Luna terra-cotta. In Fig. 79, in the bottom of the vase, the same design is drawn with symmetry, and

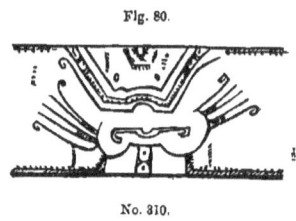

Fig. 80.

No. 310.

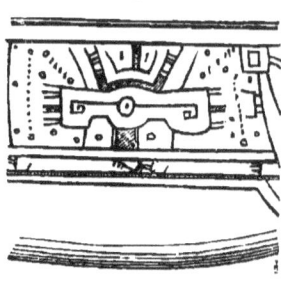

Fig. 81.

No. 22,311.

well painted, but the paint has been much effaced. In Figs. 80, 81, the figure has assumed more regularity and simplicity, still the dots and circles are utterly irregular.

Mr. Squier, in his "Serpent Symbol," illustrated an architectural ornament on a temple at Ocosingo,[*] in which a winged or plumed globe rested on the back of a conventional serpent. He compared this with a very similar design from Assyria. Comparison of the figure, which we have studied, with that of Mr. Squier, shows a marked resemblance in the radical elements. May not the conventional and awkward forms on the Luna ware have originated in an attempt to reproduce the Ocosingo design?

In No. 22,369 we have a specimen of great simplicity outside, but painted in intricate style within. The color, a dingy buff, is relieved by a brown band around the rim. Inside are five zones, the pattern in alternates being similar; making three of one and two of the other form. The lines are, in some cases, shaded with red, in others, with drab. The central panel in the bottom is of a dirty red, and the faces drab, except where the buff field shows in the spaces left for eyes and nose. The figures on each side, with a sort of

---

[*] Serpent Symbol. Squier. Page 248.

ARCHÆOLOGICAL RESEARCHES IN NICARAGUA. 35

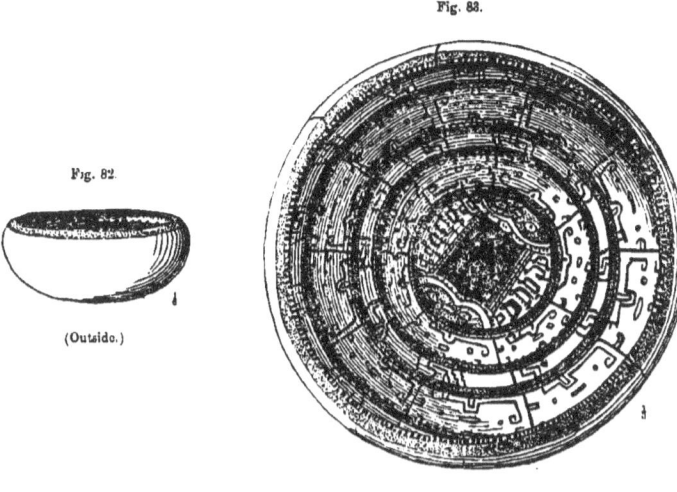

Fig. 82. (Outside.)

Fig. 83. (Inside.)

No. 22,369.—Bowl of Luna ware.

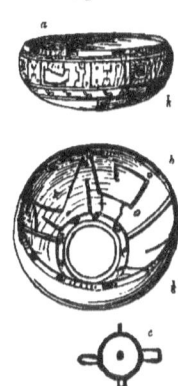

Fig. 84.

No. 22,367.—Bowl of Luna ware, cap of urn No. LXIX.

double pot-hook shape, are shaded alternately with red and drab. In the band of lines on each side of the main panel, the space between the two middle lines is in drab, the others are in red, except one, which is left in the original buff. At each end of the panel is a rude representation of a face, possibly intended for that of a monkey.

The faces mentioned are again seen in an entirely different design in the inner surface of certain bowls. The rudest specimen of this design is that in No.

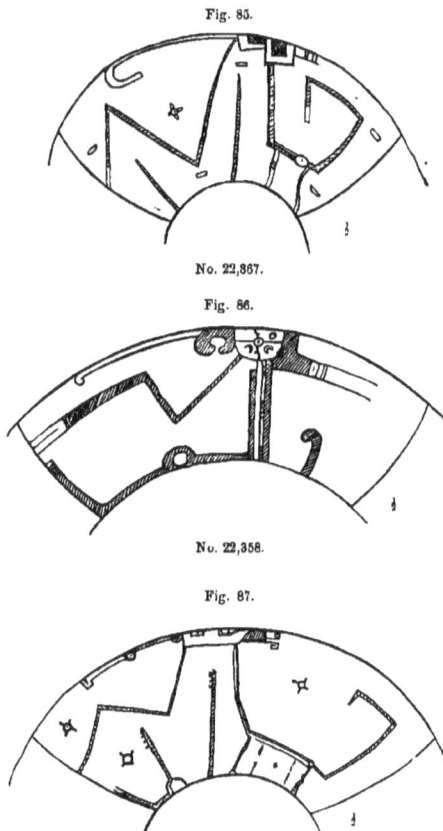

Fig. 85.
No. 22,367.

Fig. 86.
No. 22,358.

Fig. 87.
No. 310.

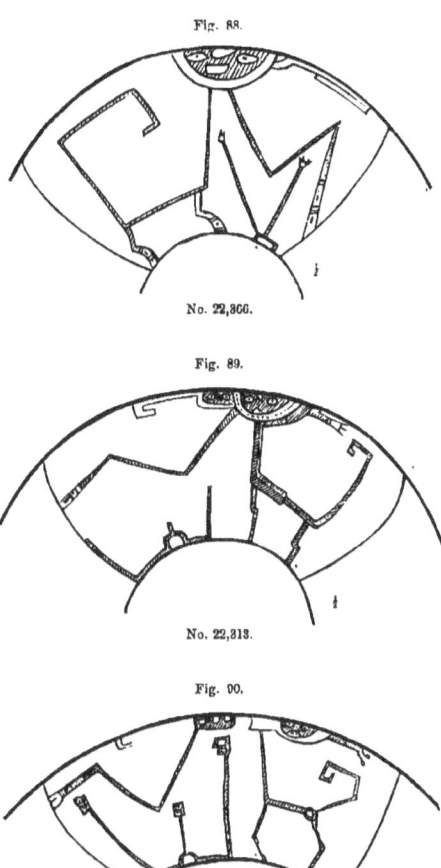

Fig. 88.
No. 22,366.

Fig. 89.
No. 22,313.

Fig. 90.
No. 209.

22,367, which was the cap to urn No. LXIX. The coloring is fresher than usual, and the outside ornamentation shows more taste than common. The two principal figures are similar and, *vis à vis*, separated by plain panels. This form is more clearly exhibited in a series through the illustrations, Figs. 86, 87, 88, 89, 90, in the last of which the limbs, the tail, and the face are suggestive of a rude delineation of a conventional monkey. The face is an improvement on its first appearance in Fig. 83, in the indication by dots of the nostrils and the pupils of the eyes.

We come now to the consideration of the faces in relief, which, in pairs, ornament fourteen specimens of the collection. These show strikingly the superiority of the manufacturers, in form, over their skill in drawing. They had good mineral paints, in light yellow, red, and brownish black, yet their highest achievement in the drawing of natural objects is that of the possible imitation of a monkey in Fig. 90. Their skill in the fictile art is well exemplified in the graceful form, Fig. 77. And here in these faces art went so far as to give some shape to the prominent features—nose, eyes, ears, and mouth—and the painter came in and, with his colors, brought the lines out in stronger relief. In several cases teeth are represented, not with great fidelity to nature, but still with a nascent regard for correct delineation. In Fig. 95, about the best of the set, instead of the irregular oval or triangle, painted over, except where spots were left for eyes and mouth, the features are in relief and painted, even to the teeth and nostrils. With these, as with other primitive people, the worker in the plastic clay had acquired considerable skill in modelling the form before he could embellish his ware with agreeable painted ornamentation.

Fig. 91.

No. 22,856.

In figure 91 may be observed a typical specimen in form and expression. The eyes are oval and elongated, and slant inward and downward. The artist was so careless as to have one eye higher than the other. The pupils are represented by dark spots. Between the eyes is a sigmoid figure, to indicate the brows or nose. The latter is raised at the point, and has a dark horizontal line in the place of the nostrils. From each corner of the mouth a broad red line or band is drawn to a point below the ears. Two others, perpendicular, are seen on the chin. If this was intended as a face and not a mask, the lines were probably the prevailing fashion of the times in tattooing or painting.

Fig. 92.

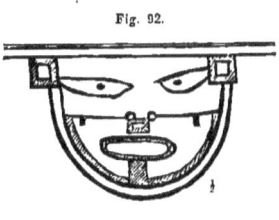

No. 22,311.

In Fig. 92 the horizontal lines were drawn from the nostrils, which are represented by rings. The tip of the nose was painted red, and on the chin and jaws are bands of the same color.

Fig. 93.

No. 22,317.

The nose in Fig. 93 is indicated by double pot-hooks. The horizontal line is in red from the corners of the mouth. The same red band is on the chin and jaws, as in the preceding illustration.

Fig. 94.

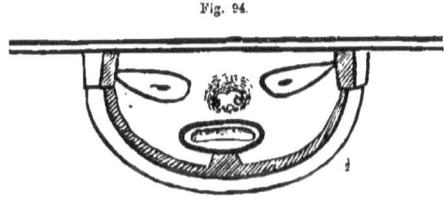

No. 22,388.

No. 22,388 is painted a dirty yellow, with heavy lines in dark red and others of light red, as shading in the mouth and on the jaws. The band on the chin is also in light red. The lips and nose are quite prominent, the nostrils indicated as usual by painted spots.

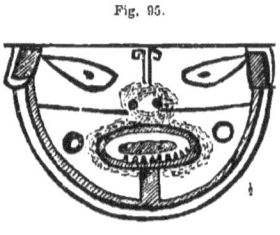

Fig. 95.

No. 22,360.

In Fig. 95 is seen about the best result in this line. The face would be a tolerable oval if the band did not cut off most of the forehead. The ears, lips, and nose are in relief; the last quite prominently so. Between the eyes and above the nose is the double pot-hook figure, apparently intended here to represent the brows. Rings stand for nostrils, and from them the horizontal lines are drawn. On each cheek below the line there is a circle. The lips have the dark lines shaded inside with red. In the middle of the mouth a red band or oval was probably intended for the tongue. The teeth are confined to the lower jaw. The usual red band is on the chin, and a red line shades the black one, which gives outline to the jaw.

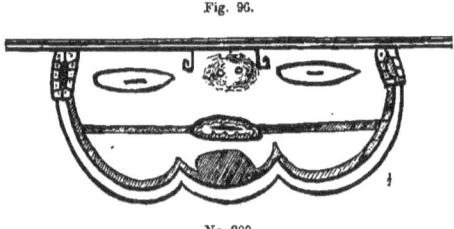

Fig. 96.

No. 299.

The irregular outline of Fig. 96 looks more like that of a mask, of great breadth, with scalloped jaws and chin. The point of the nose in relief is just between or rather above the eyes. The pot-hook is on each side of the nose, above and inverted. The horizontal band in red is here from the corners of the mouth. Another is on the chin and shading the jaws. Red shades the dark line of the lips, and prolongations or serrations of this form the teeth. The tongue is also indicated, while the ears were considered large enough to be divided into compartments.

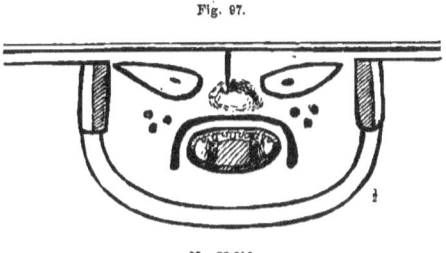

Fig. 97.

No. 22,316.

A vertical line is placed between the eyes in Fig. 97, and, instead of the horizontal, there is a heavy curved line drawn over the upper lip, in the position of a mustache, coming down on each side to the lowest level of the lips. Three spots are daubed on each cheek. On each side of a mass in the middle of the mouth is a concavity, so as to bring this tongue (?) out in relief. The latter is painted red. The dark line on the lips is shaded inside with red, and there are teeth in the upper jaw.

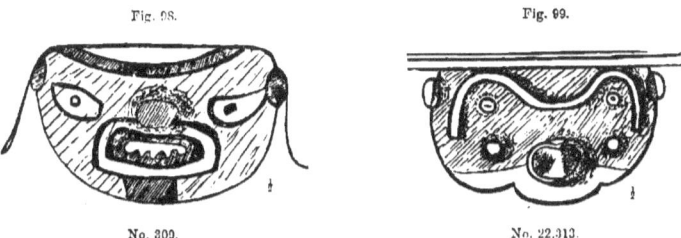

Fig. 98.   Fig. 99.

No. 309.   No. 22,313.

Fig. 98 is found on the upper end of each leg of the tripod, No. 309. It has very much the appearance of a mask. Except the eyes and a vacant space around the mouth it is all painted red; darker red being used in a band on the forehead, the ears, the tip of the nose, the chin, and the lips and teeth—the latter are only in the lower jaw. The outlines of the figure are in black. Fig. 99 is still more like a mask. Here nearly the whole face is in light red. There is no attempt at a natural shape for the eyes. The mouth pouts out in the most extraordinary manner, and there is a heavy double line raised and extending across the brow and down the cheek on each side.

There are four other specimens of this kind which are not considered worthy of individual description.

In Captain Dow's collection there is a small image of a man in this terra-cotta. It has the face found on the bowls. The top of the head is painted, as if for a head-dress, and on the back of the head are lines, evidently intended as hair. On the breast are lines of dots, terminating in small rings. At the umbilicus there is a scooped-out depression, which is painted. The arms are attached to the sides, and have five points painted on the outside of the ends for fingers. There are also painted lines or bands which are in the positions of, and may have been designed to represent, a necklace, armlets, bracelets, and a breech clout. As in the vessels of the same ware, the field color is buff, and the lines brownish black or red.

One of the prettiest pieces of the Luna ware is the plate, No. 22,357, Fig. 100. It is painted in reddish yellow, and the surface is a perfect net-work of

Fig. 100.

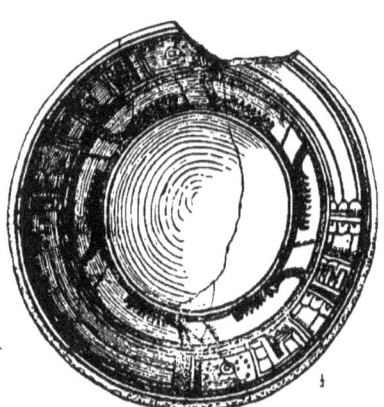

No. 22,357.—Plate of Luna terra-cotta.

the rootlet markings. One of the panels of the band around the inside is shown in Fig. 101. Below these is the band of leaf-like forms illustrated in Fig. 102. This specimen was quite well burned, well shaped, and altogether showed more skill than most vessels of the class.

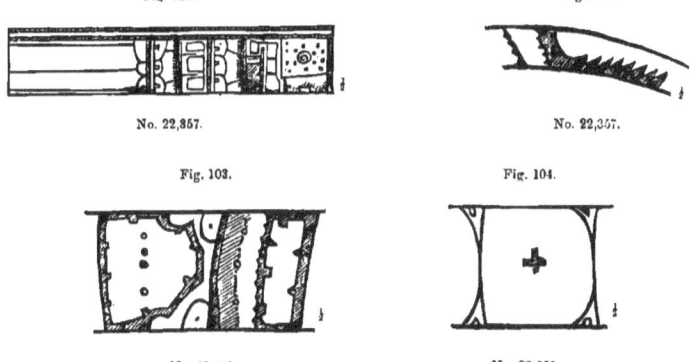

In Fig. 103 there is the panel shown in Fig. 64, modified to suit the surface of the inner side of the plate. It occurs twice *vis à vis*, with four of the simpler panels, Fig. 104, intervening.

The peculiarity of the ornamentation of this pottery adds very greatly to the interest with which it is invested by its association with the burial urns.

BLACK WARE.

In and around the burial urns were found objects in this ware tolerably well burned. It is of deep black in some pieces, and well polished. On one or both sides, where handles ought to be, are faces of monkeys or caricatured human faces, in relief. The common ornaments are incised borders, in the patterns shown in Fig. 105. The lines and dots were incised and scooped or gouged out, but in a manner to indicate considerable care and regularity in the execution of details. The articles are mostly small vessels; a few larger, pot-shaped, as if for cooking;

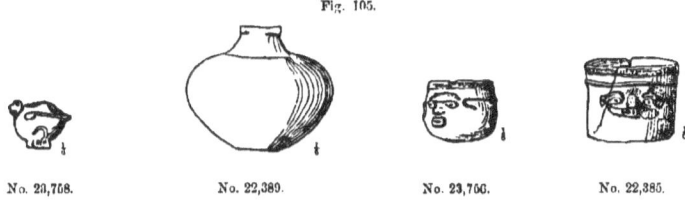

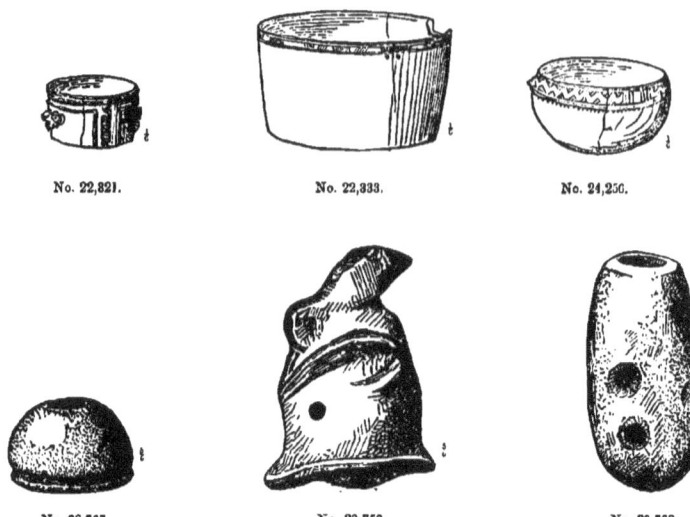

Objects in black ware from the urn burials—whistle, spindle whorl, and vessels.

and among them one in the form of a bird, and a whistle of similar shape, No. 23,759. Both of these are well formed, polished, and burned. The whistle has a compass of five notes.

CONTENTS OF THE URNS.

Besides the small articles in terra-cotta already described, the contents of the urns were human bones, remains of food, personal ornaments, and a few fragments of stone implements. The skulls were usually well shaped; but some of them were short and high, as if from slight antero-posterior compression, with heavy lower jaw and large teeth. There are a few tall Indians now living on the Madera end of the island and adjacent portion of Ometepec with the same style of countenance. The majority of the skulls were not different from those of the average Central American Indians. The bodies may have been kept out of the ground for some time, as is now done among certain Costa Rican tribes, and the desiccated remains buried. At any rate the skeleton was, as a rule, not disarticulated, but buried in a squatting posture, with the knees drawn up to the chin in the round jars, and the knees in the toe end of the shoe-shaped jars. Pieces of burnt bone were found in two instances.

In several cases there were remains of articles of food, which had been buried with the dead, in remarkably well closed urns. Among these provisions were beans, dry, but still well preserved, and seeds of different kinds, of which one resembled a grain of coffee and another charred corn. One jar had about a pint of beans and other seeds, and a piece of charcoal was in another. There were also a few shells which looked like clam shells, but were too imperfect for specific identification.

In a great many jars personal ornaments were found associated with human remains. They were usually near the bottom of the jar. Of the beads several hundred were collected, most of them of terra-cotta, pretty well burned, marked with incised lines of various designs. Next in number were pretty beads of argillite, a green stone something like nephrite but not so hard. These were drilled at each end, the holes meeting near the middle. In several urns were very fragile white beads which looked like shells, but Mr. Dall found on careful examination that they were not. There were a few beads of gold, some of which were strongly alloyed with copper and had been almost destroyed by oxidation. The metal beads were simply thin plates beaten out and rolled to form hollow

Fig. 106.

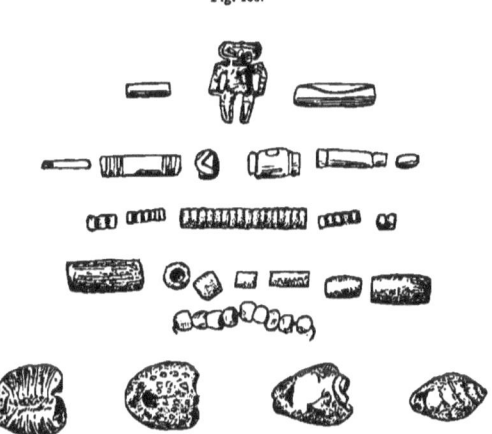

Gold image; beads of gold, terra-cotta, and argillite, (first line gold, second and third terra-cotta, fourth argillite,) and shells from the burial urns.

cylinders. A small golden image of a man was found in one jar. It was made by the curious process practiced by the Coibas at the time of the discovery,* " by soldering gold wires, drawn out into the finest threads, upon thin hammered plates of the same metal, (the plate giving the general shape and outline, the wire adding bulk, shade, and design.)" The features of the face, the fingers and toes were formed in relief by the wires. Back of the shoulders was a ring, by which it could be suspended. A larger image of similar workmanship was sent to the National Museum from Zapatera by Dr. Flint, and one from Costa Rica by Señor Zeledon. Several were received from the neighborhood of Bogota, Colombia.

In one jar an image of a frog, carved in shell, was discovered.

The following shells, identified by Mr. Dall, were found in the burial urns. They had holes for strings:

        Malea ringens, Swains.
        Trivia Solandri, Gray, (ribbed.)
        Columbella major, Sow. (smooth.)
        Oliva. Species too imperfect for determination.

A piece of flint and a fragment of a pestle were found in No. XXXIV. The flints discovered were simply chips, too crude to have been intended as instruments; they were generally of whitish chalcedony. Under CXLI was a piece of a tortilla roller. Near No. CXLV was a celt, with the cutting edge much worn. Obsidian, the *itztli* of the Aztecs, was not met with, nor was there anything like a pipe.

HACIENDA DE BALTAZA.

At this place, about two miles south of Moyogalpa, the mode of burial was similar to that at Luna's. A section of the lake bank, which was twelve feet high, is shown at page 6. The Spanish proprietor of the estate has for years collected antiquities and sold them in Rivas and Granada. From this place came most of Captain Dow's pretty collection of Ometepec pottery.

In 1877 I disinterred one large, round, flaring-rimmed jar and cap on this hacienda. It contained bones, the skull facing to the south. Near by was a small cup, ornamented with the representation of a monkey in relief. The ground had been well dug over, and fragments of round and oblong jars were strewn around in a profusion showing that great numbers had been taken out, the collector caring little for any except the small painted vessels of Luna pottery. Inland, from the line of burials, the soil contained immense numbers of fragments of the

---

* Address read before the American Geographical Society, July 10th, 1876, by Dr. C. H. Berendt.

pottery, to be described later under the head of Santa Helena, the place where it was found in largest quantity and best state of preservation. There were also chips of chalcedony and a portion of a basalt pestle. At the house little children were using the flint chips as knives to split cacao beans before planting.

Señor Baltaza had several celts which he called acrolites. He gave me two small pieces of greenish stone resembling argillite, an arrow-head of chalcedony, and a small piece of obsidian—the only specimen of it seen by me in Nicaragua. He reported celts and arrow-heads as frequently found in the ravines after heavy rains. They were often seen around the Indian huts, and one of black tremolitic rock was given me at the village.

CHILAITE.

About five miles north of Moyogalpa, at a point on the lake shore called Chilaite, antiquities were unusually abundant but a few feet above the water, on a flat between the hills and the lake. Here, within half a mile of each other, were both urn and mound burials; while between the two and around the mounds the soil was literally filled with shards and small images of the Santa Helena class. In the first—*par excellence* the Ometepec style of burial—were found the round and shoe-shaped jars, containing bones, beads, &c. Several of these urns were covered with the peculiar, fancifully painted bowls of the Luna type. The jars were imbedded in sandy soil near the lake; not in a line parallel to the present beach, but irregularly placed, as if in the sandy shore of a cove in the old coast line. The soil here was not full of shards as in the neighboring locality of the Santa Helena pottery. The jars were from eight inches to three feet below the surface. Twenty were unearthed, fifteen round and five oblong, all of which had caps. Two small black vessels were obtained; and in the jars were a few green argillite and black terra-cotta beads.

CHAPTER II.

OMETEPEC—CONTINUED.

PUEBLO VIEJO.

At the point marked A in the plan, page 8, was found the same geological formation as in Campo Santo, except that there was very little sand. The relics, pieces of pottery, were all below the lava. The latter was fifteen inches below the surface, with cobble-like stones of coarse lava a foot lower, and fragments of

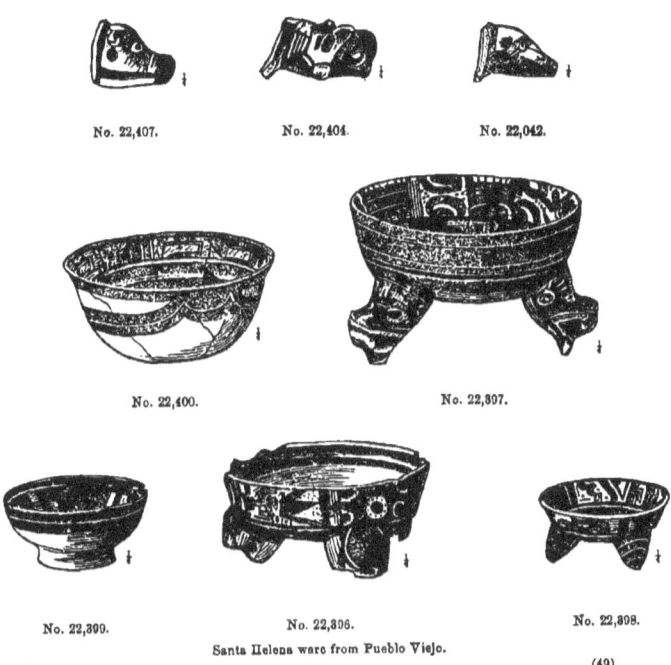

Fig. 107.

No. 22,407.   No. 22,404.   No. 22,042.

No. 22,400.   No. 22,397.

No. 22,399.   No. 22,396.   No. 22,398.

Santa Helena ware from Pueblo Viejo.

pottery in the light earth intervening. There were two sinkers made of broken pottery, one of them somewhat heart-shaped.

Some three hundred yards south of Luna's house, at a place which we christened Pueblo Viejo, the ditch for a hedge had exposed pottery shards. Besides these, stone implements, bones, &c., were discovered; all the relics being found immediately below the lava. Fragments of prettily painted pottery were taken out in great numbers. The prevailing colors were red and brown or black laid in broad bands and other designs on a field of buff or yellow.

Pieces of a mortar of coarse grained basalt and smooth roller or grinder of dolerite were obtained. Near some bones of a human skeleton was a vertebra of a shark, with a hole in its centre, which had possibly been suspended as an ornament. In several places piles of beach stones were arranged as in fire-places for cooking. Everything had the appearance as if a sudden eruption from the volcano had destroyed the huts, broken the utensils of the household, and, in some cases, overtaken the unfortunate inhabitants. The solid lava was uncovered for a space of five by seven feet. It was ten inches below the surface and five inches thick, with loose cinder above and below; while the overlying ten inches was also largely of volcanic cinder. Underlying it was a hard stratum of old ash and pebble. From under this section of lava were taken the shards marked 22,401 (Smithsonian number.) There were great numbers of similar fragments of Santa Helena pottery, but not a piece of the Luna type.

We have no means of estimating the number of years it must have required for the surface which was covered by this eruption to have become sufficiently changed to allow the gradual formation of the soil, which supported a large and prosperous population at the time of the conquest. There has been no eruption on the island since that time, and Sivers says there is no record of one within the memory of man.*

SANTA HELENA.

At a place of this name belonging to the Salgados, on the lake shore, two and a half miles north of Moyogalpa, was found by far the most beautiful pottery obtained. For convenience of reference the name of the hacienda was given to this particular type of ware. In the forest here several large trees had been blown down by the hurricane of October, 1876. Among their roots, and in the cavities formed by their uptearing, were found fragments of the painted pottery discovered before at Pueblo Viejo. In still greater numbers were shards of unpainted and imperfectly burned earthen-ware, differing from the former both

---

* Sivers' Ueber Madeira und die Antillen nach Mittelamerika, page 128.

in shape and manner of ornamentation. The interments and relics were in a line of variable width, about thirty yards from the present coast line, and in nearly the same general direction. Imbedded in a sandy formation about three feet below the surface, with a stiffer earth or clay above, these burials appear to have been made in the sand of the old lake beach, and covered later by the accumulation of soil and the wash of debris from the neighboring hills, or possibly by the ashes of a volcanic eruption, as in the section south of Moyogalpa. The soil between this line and the hills is filled to a depth of three feet with fragments of pottery, pestles, grinders, &c. These were not found in numbers of any consequence between the line of burials and the lake—another indication that the interments were originally on the old shore line; a line which, in some places, is even now varying, washing away at one point and filling in at another.

Fig. 108.

No. 28,741.—Stand for round bottomed vessels.

From the first were obtained many pieces of grinders, chalcedony chips, &c.; and, among others, several curious pieces of coarse unpainted ware, which appear to have been intended as stands for calabashes and other round bottomed vessels. There were great numbers of painted shards, many vessels of the same class, and unpainted ones of infinite variety in form and design of ornamentation. Many of the latter were oblong, their markings in some cases resembling those on the Huehuetenango urn figured by Mr. Catherwood in Stephens' work.*

The human bones were usually found with small vessels on either side and a larger one over the skull. Some of the small vessels contained bones of little animals and pieces of charcoal, in others were pieces of pumice stone, shards of painted pottery, and chalcedony chips. One of the first skeletons discovered was lying extended, with the side of the face down. During the first day's work a beautiful chipped axe of whitish chalcedony, and a red one of the same size, were obtained. Among the burials were several upright basaltic columns about three feet in height, resembling those seen later in some of the mounds and shell-heaps of Costa Rica.

As we proceeded we found that the ground, to a depth of four feet, contained many shards, sinkers made of pottery and of beach stones notched, a portion of a chalcedony spear-head, with chips of the same rock and of agate. Some of the ruder vessels were red, from better burning; while others seemed hardly to have been burned at all. Many of these were shoe-shaped, or like

---

* Stephens' Central America, Chiapas, and Yucatan, Vol. II, p. 228.

Fig. 109.

No. 28,809.

No. 28,575.

Oblong vessels from Santa Helena.

birds and other animals; and one vase, with a grotesque human head, reminds one of those described by Piedrahita, as made in imitation of the idols of the Muyscas, and used to hold their offerings of gold and emeralds. Many beautifully painted vases, usually tripods, were found, with small terra-cotta images of human beings, two of dogs, and one of an armadillo, all painted.

The shoe-shaped jars were usually small, although one measured 18 x 13 inches. This contained fragments of painted pottery and bones of some animal. Near by was a human skeleton extended, with feet to the west and arms outstretched. An alligator-shaped vase was by the head, and near the skeleton were fourteen small vessels of various shapes and sizes. The skull was rather thick and short, apparently slightly flattened behind. It was broken by the weight of the earth. Near this a jar sixteen inches long, with a broad flat cap, contained a human tooth, two small vessels, and the bones of a small animal; while in the little vessels were very diminutive bones.

In some cases large flat jars, with caps of similar description, contained skulls, small vessels, and painted fragments; while outside, the long bones were extended with feet to the west. These flat jars and caps were usually 21 inches across and 9 deep. The body was probably placed with one of the jars over and another under the head. The bones were even more fragile than those in the burial urns at Luna's—probably due to the fact that the land is lower, and they had not the protection of the well closed urns.

Fig. 110.

No. 28,442.—Bottomless vase, Santa Helena.

In one jar was a small bowl inverted and some thin pieces of young cranial bones; within the bowl were crowns of young teeth. This urn also contained a vessel shaped like a vase, which had no bottom—possibly intended to hold flowers.

The shoe-shaped jars of larger size had painted caps. Many of the specimens were in the stiffer formation above the sand—the skeletons in the sand. In one jar were bones, apparently of some animal used as food, split in a manner to suggest a supply of marrow furnished for the departed spirit on its journey to the unknown land.

The basalt columns mentioned above in no case appeared above the surface. I can imagine no use for them except as grave stones, which were covered later, although they were seen in shell-heaps and mounds in Costa Rica not rising above the surface.

In one place were found together images in terra-cotta of a man and a child, and about fifteen feet away were two females, the genitals broadly indicated. Near the latter was a skeleton, on the skull of which ninety-five sinkers of painted pottery were closely packed, as if a fisherman's net had been carefully folded and placed on his head. Over the sinkers a handsomely painted bowl was inverted. The skull was rather short and high, and seemed somewhat flattened

Fig. 111.

No. 28,479.—Tripod vase, Santa Helena terra-cotta.

behind, but otherwise well shaped. Near another skeleton was a gaudily painted tripod vase, with doves for feet. It was preserved in perfect condition, and is now in the National Museum, No. 28,479.

In a few of the larger jars were found bones of children. This mode of burial was probably borrowed from their predecessors, as was the shape of their oblong jars.

Another chalcedony axe and a spear-head of the same material were dug up, while contained in several jars, and occasionally scattered in the soil around them, were bits of red rock called *curiol* by the Indians. This they said was ground up and served as the red paint on their earthen ware. In Costa Rica black and yellow rock are also used.

Fig. 112.

No. 28,436.—Vase from Santa Helena.

The most interesting piece of pottery found was a gracefully formed vase, with figures resembling the sculpture and the stucco designs seen in the old ruins of the Maya cities, Palenque, Copan, &c. These figures seem to have been graven with a sharp instrument before the clay was burned, and then a cream colored paint applied. The paint has in many places peeled off, showing the well burned red clay beneath.

Among other objects of special interest obtained here were a spindle whorl, small painted idols, an arrow-head of chalcedony, a spear-head, a rude clay whistle shaped like a bird, two teeth of a saw-fish, and, in one of the small vessels, a shark's vertebra.

SANTA HELENA POTTERY.

Of the pottery obtained at Santa Helena the largest pieces are the flat burial jars, which were usually found over the skulls. They are about twenty-one inches in diameter and nine in depth; generally unpainted, but in some instances coated with paint of red earth, and polished, probably as at the present day, by rubbing with wet sticks or stones. These large jars usually have rims, and are tolerably well burned; on one or more sides are raised figures, in most instances the heads of monsters. Indeed, the representations on the Santa Helena pottery are generally of monsters or caricatures.

Fig. 113.

No. 28,007.   No. 28,078.

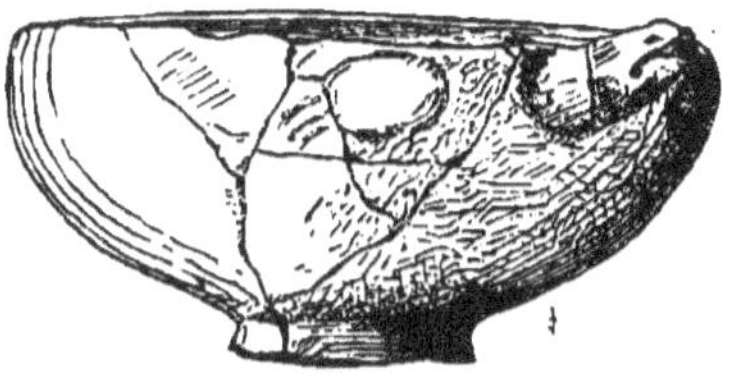

No. 28,636.

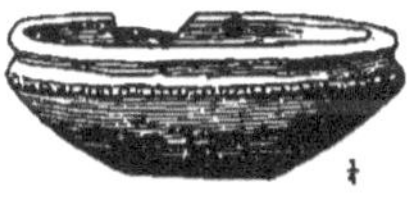

No. 28,924.    No. 28,905.    No. 28,908.

Large flat urns and fragments, Santa Helena.

Of the smaller vessels, which seem to have been designed for water and food, as shown by the remains of bones, &c., the majority are oblong, but vary infinitely in size, shape, and ornamentation, two being rarely formed alike. Evidently the potter's wheel was not used. These vessels can be arranged in a series from round to the longest oblong through an almost imperceptible gradation. A great many of them have raised ornaments on the sides and at the ends, suggesting the original bird shape, with wings, head, and tail. This form is particularly well shown in the figures of a jar from Huehuetenango, Guatemala.* From the same locality Mr. Stephens obtained other vases of Mexican style of ornamentation. A specimen of the bird-shaped jar, with head and tail, the wings indicated by painted lines, will be described as found in a mound at Los Cocos. Most of the oblong jars are unpainted, some are colored solid red, and others are marked with red on a buff ground, as if fingers dipped in red paint had been drawn along the length of the vessel. No. 28,586, Fig. 114, an oblong jar, has a head on each end, with the orifice nearly in the centre of the back. One of the heads is a monkey's, the other much like that of a seal. The latter design is quite frequent on the small end of oblong jars.

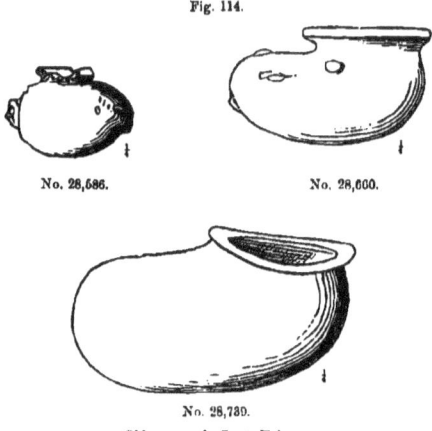

Fig. 114.

No. 28,586.   No. 28,660.

No. 28,730.
Oblong vessels, Santa Helena.

Dr. Berendt thought that the peculiar shape of the oblong burial urns was due to their convenience for containing the long bones, but the discovery of skeletons which had not been disarticulated disproved this theory. Squier noticed

---

* Central America, Chiapas, and Yucatán. Stephens. Page 231.

the skull-like form, and a resemblance to the shape of the stomach has been suggested by Professor Otis T. Mason; but, after examining hundreds of specimens, I am inclined to believe that the bird was the original type. The Luna jars probably gave the idea to the workers of Santa Helena.

In the collection there are two pieces of unpainted ware resembling the Peruvian type. One consists of two small vessels, connected by an arching handle; the other seems to have been intended as a cover, used possibly over food. It also has a long arched handle much like those on Peruvian specimens. At the junction of the handle with the body of the vessel are raised griffin-like figures. Professor Mason, who pointed out its resemblance to the Peruvian type, thinks this latter vessel may have reached Nicaragua through traffic. I only know that it was exhumed along with pre-Columbian relics.

Fig. 115.

No. 28,460.   No. 28,477.

Objects from Santa Helena, of Peruvian style.

The painted ware of Santa Helena was comparatively well burned; a little soft when unearthed, but hardening rapidly when exposed. The painting on some of this is nearly perfect still, after having been imbedded for at least three hundred and fifty years in the damp soil of tropical low-lands.

On these vessels the field is a buff or cream color, covered with figures in red, bordered with black. The prettiest tripod vase, Fig. 111, has a body a little deeper than an ordinary soup plate, with legs in the shape of doves. The bottom in the interior is taken up with what seems a conventional human face of the triangular type seen in the terra-cotta images from the ruins of Teotihuacan.[*] The interior, between the bottom and the rim, is divided into two zones by a horizontal black line. These spaces are occupied with masked human figures in profile, and following each other, as on the altar at Copan.[†] There are eight in the upper row and seven in the lower. The profuse plumes and dress ornaments also resemble many in Kingsborough's Mexican antiquities and some at Copan

---

[*] The Native Races of the Pacific States. Bancroft. Vol. IV, page 542.
[†] Central America, Chiapas, and Yucatan. Stephens. Vol. I, page 142.

and Palenque, and those on the "sacrificial stone" and the "calendar stone" dug up in the Plaza Mayor of Mexico.* Some of the figures have on sandals, and all are strikingly Aztec in style. On the outside the bottom is a solid buff color, with a red band surrounding it at the upper edge of the junction with the legs, Above this is a buff and then a black band. The space over the latter is divided into three compartments by lines above the legs. Each space contains the profile of a macaw's head, with plumes. The legs are pigeon or dove-like in shape, the breast supporting the vase, the head turned to one side, and the tail of the bird serving as a foot of the vase. The head is red, with black eyes, bordered with yellow, and the back, wings, and tail are indicated by black lines and checks.

The vase No. 28,436, which was first graven and then painted, is ornamented in a manner so intricate that any attempt at a written description would be futile. Among other figures can be distinguished the plumed serpent of Mexico and Guatemala.†

"Serpents are symbols of his (Huitzilopochtli's) mother Cohuatlycue, and also Cihuacohuatl, the serpent woman who begat twins, male and female, from which man proceeded; the same serpents and feathers are the symbols of Quezatleohuatl." ‡

Fig. 116.

No. 28,469.—Plumed serpent vase, Santa Helena.

---

* Native Races of the Pacific States. Bancroft. Vol. IV, pages 511-516. Anales del Museo Nacional de Mexico. Tomo I, Entrega 1.
† Squier's Nicaragua, Vol. I, page 406. Native Races of the Pacific States. Bancroft. Vol. IV, pages 185, 227, 513.
‡ Gallatin in the American Ethnological Society's Transactions, quoted by Bancroft in his Vol. III, page 398.

On another vase, about eight inches in height and six in diameter, are two serpents occupying nearly the whole surface on opposite sides. They are over an inch broad, painted red, with black or brown plumes on the head and either plumes or rattles, I am uncertain which, on the tail. Squier's figure from the rock painting near Managua had plumes on the tail, while that of Catherwood, from the Casa de Monjas, Uxmal, had rattles. The painting on the vase is very distinct. The gods, Quetzalcoatl in Mexico, Kukulcan in Yucatan, and Gugumatz in Guatemala, were symbolized by the plumed serpent.

In this Santa Helena mine were also found several figures, in terra-cotta, of men, women, children, and dogs, also a rude unpainted whistle, with two holes. On the man's face were red lines, giving it a tattooed appearance. One of the dogs was painted in spots, reminding one of the animals for sacrifice spoken of by the old writers. This specimen had its head turned half around, looking back. Near it a beautifully painted armadillo was found. Three boy-like images, two of them joined at the back, were found sitting astride another dog.

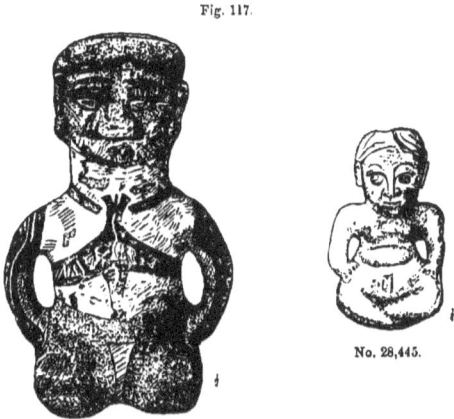

Fig. 117.

No. 28,441.
No. 28,445.
Images in terra-cotta, Santa Helena.

STONE GRAVE.

At San Francisco, on the western side of Madera, in the woods near the beach, piles of stones were pointed out as graves of the old Indians. An antique metate was shown me, which was said to have been taken from one of the heaps.

I excavated one to a depth of two feet below the general surface of the ground, but found nothing. At first I thought it would prove to be similar to the oval graves of Chiriqui, described by Dr. Merritt,* but the stones were wanting below the depth of two feet, and the earth underneath showed no signs of having been disturbed.

Near, or rather among these piles, was a hole in the ground where an armadillo pursued by boys took refuge. They began to dig for it, when human bones were found, and the hunters desisted. On examination this proved to be a stone walled sepulchre. The top was about fifteen inches below the surface; the grave being 35 inches deep, 31 inches wide, and 17 feet long. The stone slabs, from one to four inches thick, walled the sides around and covered it. One slab was 35 × 21 inches. The grave contained a small vessel of terra-cotta shaped like a duck, two other small ones of similar quality but different shape, and fragments of a large jar, which was immediately outside the wall. This pottery was of rough character, the rudest in the whole collection; still, in some places, the pieces show the remains of a surface which had been smoothed, possibly with a piece of gourd, as is done by some of the tribes of South America.† A well polished celt of tremolite and a skull were among the contents of the grave. The grave was about north and south. The northern end was paved with slabs, under which were human bones. All the bones were so very old and much decayed that I could not determine whether there were more than one skeleton.

The geological formation was of hard tenacious clay, with a great many stones of basalt.

There was considerable similarity between this grave and some of those in Tennessee, described by Dr. Joseph Jones‡ in the Smithsonian Contributions.

MOUNDS.

The village of Los Angeles is on the southern border of the llanos, as Moyogalpa is on the northern. Both are on ground higher than the cultivated belt intervening; the foot-hills on each side coming down closer to the lake. On a hill about a quarter of a mile southeastward of the village, and nearly half a mile from the lake, was a mound five feet high and thirty feet across the base. It was quite regular in form, with round base, sloping sides, and flat top. There were quite large trees growing on it; and in the centre of the top was a sink, which may have been due to the uprooting of a large tree or to excavation. We began to cut in on the surface on the north side, and carried the cut, four feet

---

* Report on the Huacals or Ancient Graves of Chiriqui, by J. King Merritt, M. D. Amer. Eth. Soc.
† Notes on the Manufacture of Pottery among Savage Races. Chas. Fred. Hartt. Page 27.
‡ Aboriginal Remains of Tennessee. 1870.

wide, nearly to the centre. On the east side we commenced on the slant about five feet from the foot, sunk a shaft below the surface level, and then cut in to the centre. Near the foot of the mound, on the north side, was a row of slab-stones, seemingly a part of an enclosure around the central portion of the mound. This wall was probably left on the east side between the foot of the mound and the shaft. One of the slabs was 30 × 25 inches and 5 inches in thickness. They were not worked, nor were those mentioned above at San Francisco. On the north side near the surface were found a small piece of greenish stone like argillite, pieces of flint and of a stone grinder and pestle in basalt, with fragments of the same class of pottery as that found at Pueblo Viejo and Santa Helena. I believe that these objects were placed in the mound at a time long subsequent to its erection. The feet and handles of the vessels were in the form of the heads of birds and other animals—hollow, and usually containing balls of baked clay

Fig. 118.

No. 22,409.—Parrot's head, Santa Helena ware from Los Angeles.

inside for rattles. In the east cut, near the centre, was a round jar with a vertebra of some small animal and a piece of charcoal.

Relics similar to those at Pueblo Viejo were dug up in the road north of the mound.

Several mounds were seen at Los Cocos, a piece of low land bordering on the lake half a mile south of Chilaite. One of them upon being opened appeared never to have been disturbed previously. It was about forty feet in diameter at the base and six feet in height. In the base, nearly four feet from the outer edge, was a corral of stones two or three feet high extending around the mound; with this exception it was of earth. Near the centre was a skeleton, with two small terra-cotta vessels. One of these, which was quite pretty, was shaped like a bird, with an opening on the back. This vessel, the probable type of the original shoe-shaped urn, was painted red, the wings being represented by buff

Fig. 119.

No. 28,584.—Bird-shaped vessel, from mound at Los Cocos.

lines on the sides. It was at the head of the skeleton, the other at the feet. A spear-head of red chalcedony and a few shards completed the contents of this mound, which was evidently erected to some departed chieftain. It required too much labor to have been expended on a single ordinary individual. In construction it was similar to the mound examined near Los Angeles. None of the mounds seen in Nicaragua had the facings of stone or cement that are so common on teocallis of Yucatan, Chiapas, and more northern Mexico.

The difference between the mounds which served as the foundation of houses and the burial mounds of Costa Rica will be mentioned later.

STONE IMAGES.

On either side of the gateway to the old church enclosure at Los Angeles was an image in basalt.

No. 1, about five feet high, was a male sitting, with a sullen, cruel expression of face; the lips thick and everted. It had a head-dress representing the head of some large animal, the face however not looking out of the mouth of the animal, as in some described by Squier, but below its chin.

No. 2, not quite so high as the other, seemed intended for a woman. It was of rougher workmanship, and much defaced. On the head was a large irregular mass shaped somewhat like a cocked hat.

Lying near one of the houses was a large head of an image, the face looking out from under what resembled a cow's head. These were all brought from a neighboring wood.

In the woods, on a hill side about one hundred yards inland from the mound, were images 3 and 4. The whole mass of No. 3 was 59 inches high. The same block of stone formed image and seat; the latter continuing 18 inches below the foot of the figure. This was a male, sitting, with his long arms hanging down by the sides of the seat. From the shoulders to the elbows a space cut through separated the arms from the body. The fingers, toes, genitals, and buttocks were well carved. The head-dress resembled a tiger's head.

No. 4, near No. 3, was a female, sitting, with a mass between the thighs, as if to represent a child *en delivrance*. The breasts, &c., were well shown. The head had been broken off.

About fifty yards inland from the last was found No. 5, a portion of a rough old image. This was close by the ruined site of a modern habitation. Near No. 5 was a well executed human head under the mask of an animal's head. It probably belonged to No. 4.

No. 6, at the foot of the mound, was a portion of a well carved figure of a young person in a half sitting position. The only part left was from the loins to the knees.

At Tierra Blanca, near the northern end of the island, I was shown an image without a head lying in the edge of the lake. Another was said to be uncovered at low water during the dry season. They were probably abandoned here after an unsuccessful attempt at embarkation.

There was a very rude small image on the beach south of Los Angeles, which had been brought from Madera. It was so rude that I could not determine whether it was intended to represent a man or a monkey.

All of these images were of basalt. There was no grace about them; the heads of all being awkwardly placed on the breast and shoulders. The Indians told of others in several places among the foot-hills of Ometepec and Madera, but seemed loth to point them out.

About a hundred yards from the mound at Los Cocos was a basalt block 53 inches high, 38 long, and 9 thick on the carved portion above ground. It was upright, with the top projecting about two feet above the surface. This part was

Fig. 120.

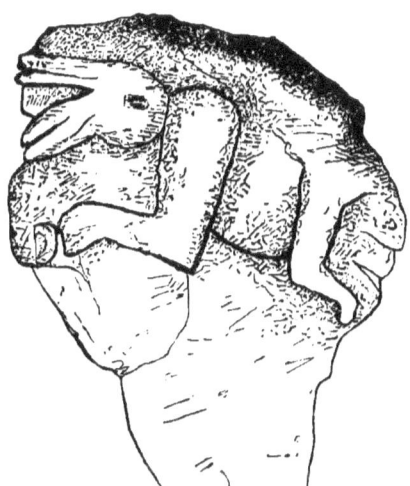

Alligator carved on basalt block.

sculptured into a representation of an alligator on the back of a man, whose head, held between the beast's fore paws, was under its throat. The head only of the man can be distinguished clearly, and it may have been intended to represent the alligator on a rock with the head in its paws.* The portion above ground had for years been used by the Indians as a grindstone to sharpen their machetes. As a consequence the monster's back had suffered, being badly worn in several places. Near by stood a small corral of basalt stones, the tops projecting above ground. Upon digging into this enclosure a portion of a stone grinder was discovered.

CARVINGS ON ROCK.

On a hillside on the southern end of the island, about a mile and a half east of Point San Ramon, are many irregular blocks of basalt with marks and figures cut on them. The hillside faces east, and is about half a mile from the lake. There were similar markings on many of the shore rocks, which, in May, were partially covered with water, notwithstanding that was about the driest season. These markings were excavated about half an inch in depth and a little more in width. Human faces and spiral lines predominated. There was also a crown, a representation of a monkey, and many irregular figures.

Block No. 1 was about four feet high, of irregular shape, with the following figures on different sides:

Fig. 121.

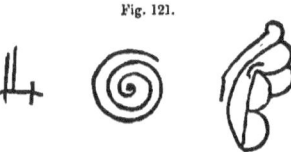

No. 2 was a rough block, some three feet in diameter, with Fig. 122 on one side.

Fig. 122.

---

* In the Museum of Natural History at New York there is a figure in clay, about five inches high, representing a human being having an alligator on the back and head, with one fore-paw on each side of the top of the head. It is in Mr. Squier's collection from Nicaragua.

No. 3 was about 4 feet thick.

It had on the west side the following:

On the north side:

On the east side:

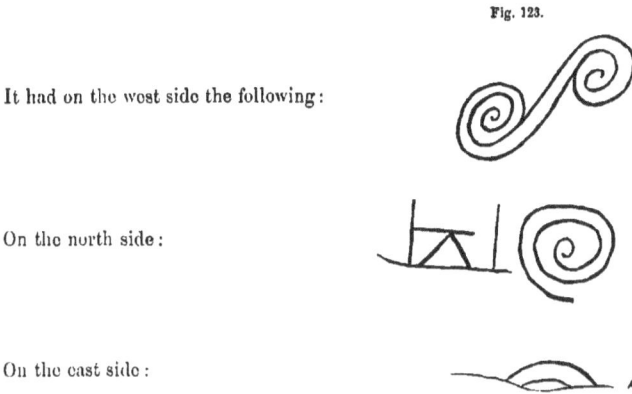

Fig. 123.

The rock was chipped off below A.

No. 4, on a rough irregular stone projecting three feet above ground, was the following figure on the south side:

Fig. 124.

No. 5, a triangular rock, had on the ridge above the surface a rude delineation of a face.

Fig. 125.

No. 6, Fig. 126, was a piece which had been chipped off.

Fig. 126.

No. 7 was much defaced, with irregular lines to the right of the figure. There was a small piece of pottery near.

Fig. 127.

No. 8.—Fig. 128.

No. 9.—Fig. 129.

No. 10.—Fig. 130.

No. 11.—Fig. 131.

No. 12.—Fig. 132.

No. 13.—Fig. 133.

Carvings on blocks of basalt, Madera.

This hill was well wooded. Down on the shore, partly under water, were numerous similar basalt blocks with many figures, faces, &c.; among them two crosses on No. 12, Fig. 132. I had to sketch sitting in a canoe, which rocked in a lively manner on the chopping waves, but the representations are sufficiently correct to give an idea of their character.

CHAPTER III.

SOME INVESTIGATIONS ON THE MAINLAND.

PALMAR.

This is a hacienda three or four miles northwest of San Jorge, on the mainland in the department of Rivas. In a field close to the lake at Palos Negros near Palmar, relics were abundant. They consisted of fragments of terra-cotta, painted in a style intermediate between the Luna and Santa Helena classes of pottery.

On the lake beach beyond, some very interesting specimens were obtained. The excavation was made during the dry season, when the water of the lake was lowest. The objects found were near the edge of the water and below its level; so that while one man dug another had to be constantly employed bailing out the water which rose rapidly in the holes. Several human skeletons were found; one with head resting on a good metate, No. 32,762, and roller. Over the skull was a bowl, inverted, and by the sides were other specimens, all of a novel variety of pottery. The vessels, bowls, and vases were formed with great regularity and grace. The ornamental lines were engraven, and the spaces intervening were painted in red, giving a curious and pleasing effect.

The bones were blackened, heavy, and well preserved. They seemed deeply impregnated with the iron, which is so conspicuous in the black sand of this beach. About a foot beneath the surface the sand was underlaid with a hard tenacious clay, in which the relics were imbedded. Two skeletons were lying parallel with the shore line, with the feet to the south.

Within three days after the rising of the water in the lake began it was impossible to work.

Fig. 134.

No. 28,915.   No. 28,918.

Vessels from Palmar.

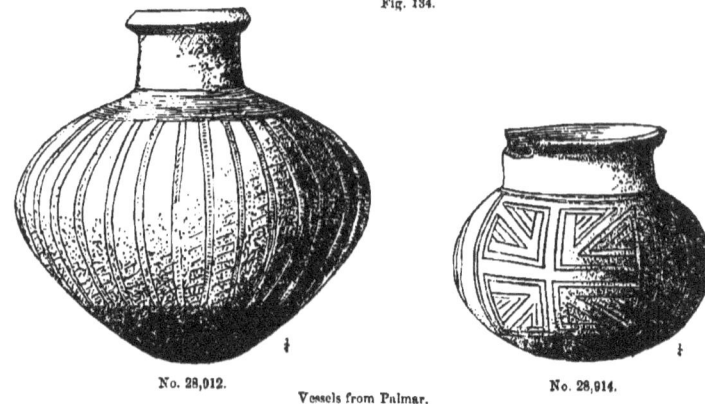

Fig. 134.

No. 28,012.   No. 28,914.

Vessels from Palmar.

MANAGUA.

While in Managua I obtained from an old woman a number of large pottery beads. One of them was much larger than the others, differently shaped, and marked with engraven characters resembling those of the so-called Runic inscriptions on the island of Monhegan.* They were reported to have been found in a jar unearthed while digging the foundation for a house in the city. These beads, No. 28,866, look like an Indian imitation of a rosary.

A small vessel in polished black ware, like that with the Luna pottery, was also shown, and I purchased a tripod vase, painted much like some of the specimens from Los Cocos and Palos Negros and others sent from Nandaime by Dr. Earl Flint. In the bottom this vessel is checked with incised lines in a manner similar to some recently received from Mexico, and said to have been used as pepper grinders.

SAN JUAN DEL SUR.

While digging post holes for the house of M. Christophle in this village, the workmen discovered specimens of antique pottery.

Other relics were reported in the woods north of the village, and, on going out with a guide among the hills in that direction, I was rewarded by finding some interesting remains. Upon a slight eminence, which overlooked a *quebrada*, were heaps of stones, portions of an old metate and roller of basalt rotten with

---

* Schoolcraft.—Indian Tribes of the United States. Vol. VI, page 611.

age, and fragments of rough pottery ornamented with pinched and dotted borders.

The surface of the neighboring low land was, in some places, covered with shards and marine shells, principally oysters, clams, and two or three varieties of volutes. This was the first appearance of kitchen-middens; but they were afterwards seen in the form of immense shell-heaps, closely set, and almost covering acres of land on the Costa Rica coast, near Nagascola, on the northwest side of Culebra Bay.

MANUFACTURE OF POTTERY NEAR SAN JORGE.

Just before leaving Nicaragua I visited a place in the environs of San Jorge where pottery was manufactured in considerable quantity. An old woman and several girls were at work; one of the girls not more than six or seven years old. The clay was taken from a cut in the road near the house, the sand from the road-bed, that of the lake shore not being considered so good. The fashioning of the pottery was begun on the bottom of other vessels, and it was then built up by the rope method. The ears and handles were added afterwards by luting. The surface was made even, first with the fingers repeatedly dipped in water, and then with a smooth stick, the latter giving quite a polish to the surface. A finer polish was obtained by rubbing with a smooth stone. Red earth was occasionally washed over vessels as a paint, and some were blackened with smoke while moist. The ware was partially dried before being burned. The articles were well made, and very pretty and graceful. Nos. 28,930–1 are modern vessels of similar make from Masaya.

CHAPTER IV.

NICOYA.

On the trail between San Juan del Sur and the Costa Rica line the hills bordering the coast are of the same trap formation as at San Juan,[*] with a heavy dip to the southwest into the Pacific. The country is rough and broken, the path being difficult even for mules in the dry season. Eleven spurs or hills from five hundred to a thousand feet high are crossed by the toilsome route. At Hostianal on this road, in the bed of the river, appeared numbers of pebbles of argillite, the material of the green stone beads of Ometepec and of many of the gorgets from Costa Rica. On the sea beach beyond they were again quite numerous. The source of supply must be in these coast mountains, from which the heavy freshets of the wet season wash them down. I was told by Dr. Flint that this mineral occurred on the transit road to Virgin Bay, but I was not able to find it there.

From the frontier to the village of Sardinal, about sixty miles, the country is fearfully broken toward the sea; while from the top of the hills a table-land gently falls away to the foot of the volcanoes, so that the drainage even in sight of the Pacific, is away from it to the valley of the Sapoa and the Tempisque. The basalt and trap here lie just beneath a thin layer of soil, which supports a scattered growth of scrub trees and bushes and a scant coating of grass. With the advent of the rains this grass carpets the plain with emerald green. The llanos throughout the year afford pasture ground for horses, cattle, and thousands of deer. Here are seen the partridge, and the quail and meadow lark of the United States. The streams are few in the dry season, but beautifully clear and cool, with well shaded banks, making a delightful contrast with the parched llanos.

On an exploring trip through this region, Dr. Earl Flint, of Nicaragua, and I made a joint collection for the Smithsonian Institution. The first specimens were obtained at El Jovo, the magnificent hacienda of a distinguished Nicaraguan family, the Hurtados. We made this place a sort of headquarters while in Costa Rica, and were entertained by Don David Hurtado with a cordiality which made us loth to leave his hospitable house.

Señor Hurtado presented several specimens. Among them were a small

---

[*] Report by Dr. D. H. Whitfield, in Report of Surveys for the Nicaragua Canal, page 20. Washington. 1874.

vase, prettily painted, a black one shaped like an aguacate, and a piece of jadeite (No. 28,992) about two inches in cubic dimensions. These were all from Culebra, a hacienda at the head of the bay of that name. The fragment of jadeite was said to have been eight inches long, but was broken by the children who had used it as a plaything.

While I was confined to the house by illness for three days, Dr. Flint visited Culebra and reported several mounds of stone seven feet in height, with many fragments of metates in basalt. He mentioned tall stones in the mounds, like the tombstones of Santa Helena, and discovered large shell-heaps in the same neighborhood.

Among the articles said to have come from these mounds were a mortar of lava, a rude vase with excrescent-like ornaments, a painted tripod, and a fragment of pottery painted green.

Near Bocarones, on the Rio Tempisque, were small heaps of stones similar in appearance to those at San Francisco. I had no time to open them, but was informed by the proprietor of the land that they were tombs, and contained metates, painted pottery, &c.

Throughout this fertile valley of the Tempisque, which is well wooded and, along the road, well cultivated, relics of the old Indians abound. This, indeed, has been the case wherever I have examined fertile spots on the Pacific slope of Central America. In many places where dense forests now stand, the mouldering leaves cover vestiges of a once teeming and prosperous population.

An old Spanish lady at Bocarones described—without the aid of leading questions—urn burials precisely similar to those at the *hacienda de Luna*, Ometepec. She said the skeletons were sitting in the urns with knees drawn up to their chins, and that in the jars and around them were small vessels, beads, burnt corn, beans, &c. The burials were on the opposite side of the river, and were shown by a son of the lady. They were in *huacas* on a hill about half a mile from the river. The hill, some fifty feet high, was one of a narrow irregular range. On the southwest edge of the summit was a parapet of columnar basalt—the columns so regular as almost to appear chiseled. There were several mounds of earth and stone, about eight feet high, on the west side of the hill, some of which had been opened, and scattered around were fragments of metates of great variety in size and ornamentation, the feet of some being twelve inches long; also many shards of pottery, some of them painted, pieces of tripods, and fragments about an inch thick of very large jars. The latter, judging by the curve of the fragments, must have been three or four feet in diameter.

Standing in a fence in the village was a basalt idol of the Zapatera style. It projected some four feet above the surface. Señor Vargas informed me that it was brought from a neighboring huaca.

In the village was purchased a greenish celt of jadeite, No. 28,991, extremely hard and exquisitely polished.

At the town of Nicoya a turtle-shaped whistle and two small vessels were obtained, and a little further south, in the valleys among the mountains, were observed many mounds and other remains of antiquity. The mounds were usually about five feet in height and forty in diameter at the base. In the road cuts and gullies fragments of stone implements and terra-cotta were abundant. A piece of a fine long celt of tremolite was lying in a rut, broken by a cart wheel. We purchased two whistles and some little vessels in this neighborhood, and were shown the locality where they had been discovered with human bones and several metates. I employed four men at work there for half a day, and

Fig. 135.

No. 28,952.　　　　　　　　No. 28,953.
Whistles exhumed at Nicoya.

unearthed three whistles, four small vessels, and bones of several skeletons. Each body appeared to have been interred with a small earthen vessel and a whistle. This place, about a mile and a half southeast of the town, where the crest of the ridge was crossed by the road, was called Punta del Monte. The specimens were lying in red clay, on a yellowish trap or *cascaja*, about four feet below the surface; and had been exposed, in a cut in the road, by the wash of the rainy season. Throughout this country the metates are dug up for sale. They are considered more valuable than those now made, and bring from six to eight dollars.

The remaining half day the men worked in the mounds half a mile farther south. Two were cut into, showing great numbers of shards, pieces of grinders, and *curiol*. Human bones were found once; but I think they were placed there subsequently to the erection of the mound. The natives said that metates, but no bones, were found in the mounds. They seemed to have been built as the sites of houses, the debris of household utensils gradually accumulating on the mound foundation. There were very few stones, which were scarce in the immediate neighborhood.

A magnificent chalchihuitl, No. 28,977, was obtained near here, and Dr. Flint purchased for himself an opal, with a perforation in it like those drilled in the green beads of Ometepec.

A narrow vein of hard black rock was pointed out by the Indians as a source of black paint. Flint of great variety in color abounded in the mountains, and I saw a vein of very pretty heliotrope, blood-stone. Urn burial was reported, but not seen.

The inhabitants of the town of Nicoya are light colored *mestizos*, generally indicating more Spanish blood than is seen in the average Nicaraguan. In the mountains there are some pure-blood Indians. Sugar, corn, and plantains flourish in the valleys; while the woods, according to the natives, yield fruit for man's food the entire year. The cacao tree grows wild.

On our return several ornaments in green stone were obtained at Sardinal. Of these, two flat gorgets, a ball with perforations for a string, and an amulet with a human face engraved on one side, were of the mineral called argillite, of beautiful green color, but much softer than jade. There was a fragment of an amulet or gorget of jadeite, No. 28,990, and what seemed the figure of a woodpecker, No. 28,978, in a greenish serpentine; also a turtle, No. 28,979, in a curious marble-like green stone, and a black celt of volcanic rock.

Huacas were noticed on the hills in every direction, and two large basalt idols were reported near Panama and others at Santa Rosa.

Some of the painted fragments of pottery from Nagascola, in their markings more closely resembled the Luna pottery than any other seen. The paint was much effaced and the lines uncertain. We had many apparently reliable reports of a vein of green rock in the hills near this place, but personal investigation met with disappointment.

On the northwest side of Culebra Bay, between it and the ocean, extends a narrow peninsula, in a gorge on the bay side of which is a small level space of three or four acres. Shell-heaps, in some places six feet high, nearly cover this space. Among the shells were many fragments of pottery, pieces of metates, celts, stone axes, &c. Some of the painted terra-cotta resembled the Luna type. The shells were of great variety, though principally oysters, clams, and volutes. A native who lived there said that human bones were found in the heaps. In one an excavation had been made, and basalt pillars were shown, like those in a mound at Culebra reported by Dr. Flint, and some before mentioned at Santa Helena. These were said to mark the positions of the skeletons. They did not project above the surface. There was neither regularity nor symmetry in these heaps, which were evidently kitchen-middens formed by the gradual accumulation of shells.

The little valley was extremely fertile, easily defended, and formed an admirable location for a village in troublous times. On the hill, which was about five hundred feet in height, there were other shell-heaps.

ARCHÆOLOGICAL RESEARCHES IN NICARAGUA. 77

OBJECTS IN GREEN STONE.

The collection made by Dr. Flint and myself in Costa Rica contains sixteen objects in green stone, chalchihuitls. First is No. 28,977, a large gorget or breastplate shaped like that called a hatchet by Squier.* It is of jadeite, finely polished, and on one side elaborately engraved with the representation of a man. It is difficult to conceive how such results could have been accomplished on this extremely hard stone without iron tools. True, the ancient Americans had instruments of very hard bronze; and we well know the wonderful results still achieved by the patient Indian with his drill of wood or reed and sand and water.† Squier saw an Indian of Central America working in that manner.

Next comes No. 28,991, a beautiful celt of light green jadeite of great hardness, but wonderfully polished. No. 28,987 is a thin jadeite amulet three quarters of an inch wide and not quite four inches long, with a hole for suspension. The fine polish shows well the mottled graining of this specimen. No. 28,989 is an irregular, lozenge-shaped amulet of clear green jadeite. In one end is a small hole, drilled. No. 28,990, a fragment of a jadeite amulet, is a very pretty specimen of the mineral, in appearance much like the unworked piece, No. 28,992, obtained at Culebra. The latter is 2½ × 2½ × 2 inches, of handsome light green jadeite. The top and one end are smooth, like polished pebble; the bottom and one side were apparently sawed, possibly with copper wire and sand;‡ the remaining end and side show fracture. It looks as if the workman had sawed down into a smooth block to the depth of about two inches, then cut horizontally about the same distance, leaving the piece attached only at one side, finally breaking it away by blows with a mallet. This violence probably cracked the piece badly, as it was at first about eight inches long, according to the report of the gentleman by whom it was presented, but was broken by the children, whose plaything it was. A chip about half an inch thick, which was nearly separated by a crack when we obtained it, has since become detached.

No. 28,982, a bead of dark green jadeite from Sardinal, is an inch and three quarters long, and looks something like the jade ornament which holds the feathers in the hat of a Chinese mandarin.

No. 28,983 is an argillite bead two inches long. Numbers 28,980, 28,984, 28,985, 28,986, and 28,988 are all amulets in argillite. The first of them has on one side a rude graven representation of a human figure. No. 28,981 is the argillite ball from Sardinal, an inch in diameter, with a hole drilled a third of

---

* The American Naturalist. May, 1870. Pages 180, 181.
† See Prof. Charles Rau in Smithsonian Report, 1868, page 393. For account of stone drills found in New Jersey see paper by Dr. Abbott, Smithsonian Report, 1876, page 320.
‡ Professor Pumpelly thinks that the jadeite was probably so cut.

the way through, and two smaller ones leading diagonally into the first from the sides—an ingenious manner of making a perforation for suspension without drilling entirely through the ornament.

The turtle, No. 28,979, has a hole in one forefoot and one hindfoot, and must have been worn suspended side up. It is of green marble. The woodpecker, parrot, or some other bird, in serpentine is No. 28,978.

Green appears to have been the sacred color with the aborigines from Arizona to Peru. Throughout this region green stone ornaments were found by the Spaniards to be objects held in the highest estimation. Sahagun says that the common people of Mexico were not allowed to wear them.* The Aztecs' knowledge of mineralogy was not sufficient to enable them to make fine distinctions in the character of material; and in Mexico the term chalchihuitl seems to have been applied to all pretty green stone susceptible of high polish. The god Quetzalcoatl taught the art, and was the patron of the workers in chalchihuitl. The divinity worshipped by the fishermen, the goddess Chalchihuitlicue, is described by Clavigero as the goddess of water, clothed in a green robe of chalchihuitls.†

Persons who have been in the tropics at the close of the dry spell, when vegetation was parched and dying, and have seen the whole face of nature rejuvenated by the first showers of the rainy season—the dry llanos transformed as by magic into lawns of freshest green—can well understand how water came to be a synonym for life, and green the color in which its goddess was clothed.

The fact that at the same season the serpents come out in great numbers and gorgeous coats may help to account for their symbolic significance. On the trip to Costa Rica, during the dry season, although riding through the wildest country for more than two weeks, not a snake was seen; after the first rain they were observed in great numbers.

---

* Squier in American Naturalist. May, 1870. Page 178.

"Le culte de l'émeraude n'existait pas à la Nouvelle Granade : mais on attribuait à cette pierre une origine céleste." (Saffray. Voyage à la Nouvelle Granade, La Tour du Monde, 1873.)

Some of the old Spanish chroniclers speak loosely of all green stone ornaments as emerald, as in the frequent allusions made to this mineral by Piedrahita and Simon in their writings recording the conquest of Columbia. (See articles of Ternaux-Compans on Cundinimarca, Nouvelles Annales des Voyages, 4ᵐᵉ série, 6, 7, 8.)

† Bancroft. Native Races of the Pacific States, Vol. III, page 368.

CHAPTER V.

CONCLUSION.

In an attempt at a chronological arrangement of the antiquities of Ometepec it will be more convenient to begin at the time of the conquest with the material which history affords, and work back as well as we may with the aid of tradition, philology, and archæology.

The Spanish chroniclers record the fact that this department of Rivas was in a thriving condition, and peopled by a dense population engaged in peaceful pursuits. The authorities are pretty well agreed that the inhabitants were of kindred stock to the Aztecs of the valley of Mexico. Dr. Berendt, through his researches in southern Mexico, Guatemala, and Nicaragua found remnants of language confirming the traditions which were preserved by the natives after the discovery. He gives the following condensation of these legends:

" From the comparison of the somewhat obscure traditions preserved principally by Oviedo, Torquemada, and Herrera, it seems to result that the people in question first inhabited the ancient city of Cholula, on the famous table-lands of Mexico called Anahuac, and that from this city they were named Cholutecas, or, with a corruption, Chorotegas; that afterwards, being pressed by their neighbors, they emigrated to the southeast and settled in the deserts between Tehuantepec and Soconusco." " Attacked by their old enemies, they migrated still further to the south, and finally settled on the strip of land between the Nicaragua lakes and the Pacific, occupying the coast from Fonseca Bay to Nicoya. But even here they were not destined to remain unmolested. Another invasion by a tribe of the Nahuatl stock took place, and this time the invaders, wedging themselves right into their midst, got possession, and that permanently, of what is now the department of Rivas in Nicaragua, from which they likewise peopled the islands of the great lake."*

Squier's investigations as late as 1850 showed the remains of the Aztec language on the island of Ometepec.

The people found here by the Spaniards buried the dead of the common people, with their ornaments and utensils, in the fields, gardens, or even under

---

*Address read before the American Geographical Society July 10, 1876.

the floor of their huts. The grandees had the distinction of cremation, and their ashes were buried in urns.*

The mode of burial at Santa Helena was that described for the poorer people, and that such was their pecuniary condition was indicated by the absence of rich ornaments in gold or green stones, and the comparative scarcity of the fine terra-cotta, fragments of which were found in the vessels, as if they had been particularly prized. The style of painting has been described as Aztec. I have seen this terra-cotta from no place except Ometepec. A class of painted ware resembling it to a certain extent, and seemingly intermediate between it and the Luna, was found at Los Cocos on the island, and on the mainland at Palos Negros and Managua. Dr. Flint has sent specimens of the latter class from Zapatera, Nandaime, Granada, and Nindiri—all within the territory occupied by the Chorotegas, whose work it probably was.

The Santa Helena ware was found at Pueblo Viejo under a solid crust of the old lava or cinder. On the results of the last eruption was a soil which, at the time of the conquest, supported a large population. Oviedo says there were nine villages on the island.† It must have required long years for the soil to form, the Indians to lose their dread of the volcano sufficiently to live in such an exposed position, and, finally, for the growth of the population. So at least a century may well be believed to have passed between the time of the latest eruption and the occupation of the country by the Spaniards. The great numbers of the relics at Pueblo Viejo, Los Angeles, and other places, indicate a large population prior to the occurrence of the volcanic eruption.

Antedating this era was that during which the Chorotegas occupied the country. Of the extent of the latter period we have no means of forming an opinion.

The period of the Luna pottery and the burial urns was anterior to the time of the Chorotegas, immediately, possibly, but of this also we lack evidence. The people of Santa Helena borrowed of them the form of the shoe-shaped jars, but the pattern may have been taken from burials even then ancient. The Luna terra-cotta has only been found in burial places on the island of Ometepec, a fact which led Friedrichsthal to think that this was used as a grand cemetery for people living on the mainland. Boyle figures two specimens from Chontales,‡ but as he does not mention how he obtained them, it is probable they were stray pieces from Ometepec. In the painting on this pottery there is no appearance of figures resembling the styles of the Aztecs or Mayas, except the possible similarity pointed out between figure 116 and the design from the temple at Ocosingo.

---

* Oviedo.—Historia General y Natural de las Indias, Tom. IV, page 48.
Bancroft.—Native Races of the Pacific States, Vol. II, page 800.
† Oviedo.—Historia General y Natural de las Indias, Tom. IV, page 63.
‡ Boyle.—A Ride across a Continent, Vol. II, page 96.

Attempts at the painting of natural objects are not noticed except in the rude faces and the monkey-like figures. Considering the activity and enterprise of the Mexican merchants, it is probable that the art of contemporary people in Nicaragua was influenced by the styles in vogue in Anahuac. The lack of this influence on the Luna ware is, therefore, evidence that it was more ancient than the Nahua civilization. The use of green stone increased as the Spaniards went south into Colombia. The gold image from the burial urn is of the peculiar workmanship found in Panama and Bogota, but, so far as I know, not seen north of Nicaragua. Dr. Berendt informed me that the shoe-shaped urns were discovered in Guatemala and in the interior of the United States of Colombia by Professor Bastian, of Berlin. Burial in urns was a custom prevalent to a certain extent throughout the northern portion of South America and the region drained by the Amazon.*

These facts, taken in connection with the absence of the enormous pyramids, temples, and palaces, with the elaborate sculptures, picture-writing, and hieroglyphics of the north, indicate that, prior to the arrival of the Chorotegas in this country, the people were more closely connected with the South Americans than with the Nahuas and Mayas of Mexico and Guatemala.

That the mounds were built prior to the time of the Aztecs of Santa Helena and the Chorotegas is proved by the fact that they were found in the midst of relics of these peoples, while the body of the mound, in each case, was free from their remains. The shards of Santa Helena terra-cotta found in the mound at Los Angeles were near the surface, and had evidently not been there prior to or at the time of its erection.

The pottery of the stone sepulchre was greatly inferior to that of the mounds.

---

* Hartt in the American Naturalist. July, 1871. Page 250 et seq.

"D'Orbigny speaks of the large earthen vessels in which the dead of the tribe, Guarayos, were buried," (in Bolivia.) Notes on the Manufacture of Pottery among Savage Races, page 40. Hartt.

Franz Keller.—The Madeira and the Amazon, page 40.

Von Martius, in Beiträge zur Ethnographie und Sprachenkunde Amerikas, Vol. I, page 440, in speaking of the Omaguas, says: "They also manufactured clay vessels of a large size, so that the corpses of their chiefs and the heads of families could be buried in them in their huts. This belongs to those arts which cannot be ascribed to all tribes. Fragments of such burial vessels have been exhumed near Manaos (formerly Villa de Barro do Rio Negro,) Fontaboa, Sapa on the Rio das Trombetas, and other localities along the principal streams." Page 177: "The Tupis have no funeral monuments. They used to bury erect, in a sitting or squatting posture—thighs against the abdomen—hands crossed under the chin over the breast, the bodies unencumbered, or in earthen vessels. They raised no tumuli, and had no common burial places. The urns were quite simple and without ornament, and were of baked reddish clay. They were buried shallow, and without special measures of protection."

In her work, "The Ceramic Art," Miss Young quotes Ewbank on the burial urns in Brazil, and figures one on page 414.

Humboldt mentions burial urns in New Granada, in Vues des Cordillères.

In "Antiquities of the Southern Indians," page 456, Col. Chas. Jones describes the discovery of the bones of a child in an earthen vessel in Georgia.

In fact, it was the rudest found on the island, and probably belongs to a remote antiquity.

The large stone images were usually found in pairs, male and female. This was the case in New Granada and Mexico. The masks of animals' heads show a resemblance to Mexican styles; but there is a grim simplicity and massiveness in their appearance, very different from the elaborately and curiously ornamented idols of the Aztecs. Dr. Berendt told me he had never seen similar statues north of Nicaragua. Mr. Squier saw two images at Tiahuanuco* which reminded him strongly of those which he had carefully studied in Central America, and described in his work on Nicaragua. The only figure of an image of the Muyscas that I have seen had much more regular features than those of Ometepec.†

The rock inscriptions of Madera are rude pictographs, in which the human face frequently occurs. Dr. Berendt considered the basalt blocks as somewhat after the order of tombstones, where the faces of the deceased were supposed to be represented. The wear on the hard rock, which seems to have been only the result of time and weather, is enough to impress the beholder with an idea of great antiquity. I think they long antedate the rock inscriptions and paintings near Managua. described by Squier, and those so common on the rocks of northern Mexico and some of the Territories of the United States. Schomburgk, quoted by Sivers, mentions inscriptions on the island of Saint Thomas, West Indies, of somewhat similar character to those of Nicaragua.‡ The inscriptions which were figured above resemble those in the State of Panama described by Seemann, and compared by him to some in Northumberland, England.§ Humboldt gave accounts of numerous inscriptions on the Essiquibo and the Orinoco, and some similar to those of Madera were noticed on the Amazon by Hartt.|| It will be observed that a great portion of the region in which this class of inscriptions has been discovered coincides pretty well with territory, at one time or another, occupied by the Caribs. There is nothing in their character to show identity of origin with either of the classes of pottery described.

To the student of American archæology there can be no more interesting field for research than Nicaragua. Here was the debatable land between North and South America, between Mayas and Aztecs on one side and Muyscas or Chibchas on the other, and, as a third grim factor, the savage of the Atlantic coast occasionally stepped in to dispute supremacy with his more civilized but

---

* Squier.—Peru. Page 207.
† Humboldt.—Vues des Cordillères. Planche 44.
‡ Sivers' Ueber Madeira und die Antillen nach Mittelamerika, page 133.
§ Pim & Seemann's Dottings, page 28.
|| American Naturalist. May, 1871. Page 146 *et seq.*
The Madeira and the Amazon. Franz Keller.

less warlike neighbors. Over this whole region may be observed the marks left by the ebb and flow of the tide of conquest, and we may hope, by diligent investigation and study of the relics in which the country so abounds, to contribute something towards the unraveling of the series of prehistoric events in America.

CATALOGUE OF THE COLLECTION.

The following list gives first the Smithsonian number, then the article, the place of origin, and finally the letter P where the specimen was presented or purchased; where no P occurs the articles were dug up under the writer's supervision.

No.	Article	Origin
22,303	Earthen ware	Ometepee.
22,304	"	"
22,305	"	"
22,306	"	Santa Dominga, "
22,307	"	"
22,308	"	"
22,309	"	"
22,310	Vase	Luna hacienda, "
22,311	Bowl	" "
22,312	"	"
22,313	"	Luna hacienda, "
22,314	"	" "
22,315	"	"
22,316	"	Luna hacienda, "
22,317	"	" "
22,318	Earthen ware vessel, broken	"
22,319	" " "	"
22,320	Round urn	Luna hacienda, "
22,321	Cup, black ware	" "
22,322	Saucer, "	" "
22,323	"	"
22,324	Bowl, black ware	Luna hacienda, "
22,325	" "	" "
22,326	" "	" "
22,327	Earthen vessel	"
22,328	" black ware, Luna hacienda, "
22,329	" " " "
22,330	" " " "
22,331	"	"
22,332	"	Luna hacienda, "
22,333	" black ware, " "
22,334	"	"
22,335	Small bowl, black ware	Luna hacienda, "
22,336	Vase, " " "
22,337	Vessel, " " "
22,338	" " " "
22,339	" " " "
22,340	" broken, "	"
22,341	"	"
22,342	"	"
22,343	Oblong urn	Luna hacienda, "
22,344	Vessel, black ware	"
22,345	" "	"
22,346	"	"
22,347	"	"
22,348	" black ware	"
22,349	Vase	Luna hacienda, "
22,350	Small bowl, black ware	" "
22,351	Vessel, "	"
22,352	Plate	Luna hacienda, "
22,353	Plate	Luna hacienda, Ometepee.
22,354	Bowl	" "
22,355	Small oblong vessel	" "
22,356	Bowl	" "
22,357	Plate	" "
22,358	Bowl	" "
22,359	Vessel	" "
22,360	Deep bowl	Luna hacienda, "
22,361	Cap of large urn	" "
22,362	Vessel	"
22,363	Cap of large urn	Luna hacienda, "
22,364	Vessel	"
22,365	Bowl	Luna hacienda, "
22,366	"	" "
22,367	"	" "
22,368	Vessel	"
22,369	Bowl	Luna hacienda, "
22,370	Vessel	"
22,371	Bowl	Luna hacienda, "
22,372	Dish, black ware	" "
22,373	Bowl	" "
22,374	Vase	" "
22,375	"	" "
22,376	"	" "
22,377	Bowl	" "
22,378	"	" "
22,379	Cup	" "
22,380	Vessel	
22,381	Bowl	Luna hacienda, "
22,382	Vessel	"
22,383	"	"
22,384	Oblong urn	Luna hacienda, "
22,385	Cup, black ware	" "
22,386	Vessel, "	" "
22,387	Burial urn	"
22,388	Bowl	Luna hacienda, "
22,389	Vessel, black ware	"
22,390	"	"
22,391	"	"
22,392	"	"
22,393	"	"
22,394	Oblong urn	Luna hacienda, "
22,395	Tripod vase	"
22,396	Vessel	"
22,397	"	"
22,398	Tripod vase	"
22,399	Bowl	"
22,400	Earthen cap of urn	Luna hacienda, "
22,401	Vessel	"
22,402	"	"

(85)

CATALOGUE OF THE COLLECTION—Continued.

No.	Description	Locality
22,403	Vessel	Ometepec.
22,404	"	"
22,405	"	"
22,406	"	"
22,407	"	"
22,408	"	"
22,409	"	"
22,410	"	"
22,411	Fragment of an image	"
23,756	Vessel, black ware	Luna hacienda, "
23,757	" "	"
23,758	" bird-shaped, black ware,	"
23,759	Whistle "	"
23,760	Vessel, black ware	"
23,761	"	"
23,762	" black ware	Luna hacienda, "
23,763	"	"
23,764	"	"
23,765	" small	"
23,766	Bowl, black ware	Luna hacienda, "
23,767	Earthen ware	"
23,768	Spindle whorl, black ware	"
23,769	" "	"
23,770	Celt, from stone sepulchre	"
23,771	"	"
23,772	"	" P.
23,773	"	"
23,774	"	Luna hacienda, "
23,775	Stone hammer	"
23,776	Discoidal stone	"
23,777	"	"
23,778	Lava pestle	"
23,779	Pestle, broken	"
23,780	Leg of metate	"
23,781	Fragments of metate	"
23,782	Stone implements and fragments	"
23,783	Human teeth and bones	"
24,784	Shell ornaments (large olivæ)	"
23,785	Fragments of mortar and grinding stone	"
23,786	Mortar	"
23,787	Handle, broken	"
23,788	Fragments of rubbers or pestles	"
23,789	Sinkers of pottery	A, Luna hacienda, "
23,790	Pottery	"
24,791	Flint chips	"
23,792	23 pottery beads	Luna hacienda, "
23,793	Pottery beads	" "
23,794	38 pottery beads	" "
23,795	33 "	" "
23,796	31 "	" "
23,797	73 "	" "
23,798	Pottery beads	" "
23,799	"	" "
23,800	"	" "
23,801	40 small white beads	" "
23,802	Argillite and pottery beads,	" "
23,803	" "	" "
23,804	14 pottery beads	" "
23,805	14 "	" "
23,806	46 pottery beads	Luna hacienda, Ometepec.
23,807	117 small white beads	" "
23,808	13 pottery beads	" "
23,809	22 "	" "
23,810	Pottery beads	" "
23,811	12 small white beads	" "
23,812	75 pottery beads	" "
23,813	45 "	" "
23,814	52 "	" "
23,815	91 "	" "
23,816	28 "	" "
23,817	54 "	" "
23,818	24 "	" "
23,819	11 "	" "
23,820	8 "	" "
23,821	23 "	" "
23,822	Pottery and small white beads,	" "
23,823	" " "	" "
23,824	Small white beads	" "
23,825	Copper and gold beads	" "
23,826	Small argillite bead	" "
23,827	4 pottery and two argillite beads,	" "
23,828	Argillite beads	" "
23,829	45 "	" "
23,830	86 "	" "
23,831	22 "	" "
23,832	Argillite beads	" "
23,833	27 argillite and two gold beads,	" "
23,834	67 argillite and one large gold bead,	Luna hacienda, "
23,835	128 "	" "
23,836	Shell and gold bead	" "
23,837	Small gold image	" "
23,838	Image of a frog, in shell	" "
23,839	Beans and seeds	" "
23,840	Shell ornament	" "
23,841	Charcoal from burial urns,	" "
24,255		Nicaragua.
24,256		"
24,257		"
24,258		"
24,259		"
24,260		"
24,261		"
28,426	Pottery, painted fragment, Baltaza hacienda,	Ometepec.
28,427	" " "	" "
28,428	" " "	" "
28,429	" " "	" "
28,430	" globular vessel	" "
28,431	" leg of a vessel	" "
28,432	" " painted,	" "
28,433	Flint chips	" "
28,434	Fragment of pottery, painted,	" "
28,435	Small pestle of lava	" "
28,436	Vase, incised and painted	Santa Helena, "
28,437	Vase	" " P.
28,438	Pottery vase	" " P.
28,439	"	" "

ARCHÆOLOGICAL RESEARCHES IN NICARAGUA.

CATALOGUE OF THE COLLECTION—Continued.

Number		Description	Location		Number		Description	Location	
28,440	Pottery	vase	Santa Helena, Ometepec.		28,498	Pottery	dish, small	Santa Helena, Ometepec.	
28,441	"	image	"	"	28,499	"	bowl, small	"	"
28,442	"	vase	"	"	28,500	"	dish, small	"	"
28,443	"	vessel	"	"	28,501	"	vase, tripod	"	"
28,444	"	image	"	"	28,502	"	bowl	"	"
28,445	"	image of a woman	"	"	28,503	"	"	"	"
28,446	"	small vase	"	"	28,504	"	dish	"	"
28,447	"	image of a bird	"	"	28,505	"	bowl, small	"	"
28,448	"	cup	"	"	28,506	"	dish	"	"
28,449	"	bowl	"	"	28,507	"	bowl	"	"
28,450	"	small vase	"	"	28,508	"	vase, tripod	"	"
28,451	"	bowl	"	"	28,509	"	bowl	"	"
28,452	"	"	"	"	28,510	"	"	"	"
28,453	"	"	"	"	28,511	"	"	"	"
28,454	"	double image	"	"	28,512	"	"	"	"
28,455	"	image	"	"	28,513	"	"	"	"
28,456	"	"	"	"	28,514	"	"	"	"
28,457	"	"	"	"	28,515	"	"	"	"
28,458	"	" of a dog, (on which were seated 28,454 and 28,457) Santa Helena,	"		28,516	"	vase, tripod	"	"
					28,517	"	bowl	"	"
28,459	Pottery tripod vase		"	"	28,518	"	vase, tripod	"	"
28,460	"	cover	"	"	28,519	"	"	"	"
28,461	"	vessel	"	"	28,520	"	basin	"	"
28,462	"	"	"	"	28,521	"	bowl	"	"
28,463	"	"	"	"	28,522	"	vase, tripod	"	"
28,464	"	small globular vessel,	"	"	28,523	"	bowl	"	"
28,465	"	vase	"	"	28,524	"	vase	"	"
28,466	"	"	"	"	28,525	"	bowl	"	"
28,467	"	"	"	"	28,526	"	vase	"	"
28,468	"	"	"	"	28,527	"	"	"	"
28,469	"	"	"	"	28,528	"	"	"	"
28,470	"	" tripod	"	"	28,529	"	" tripod	"	"
28,471	"	"	"	"	28,530	"	bowl	"	"
28,472	"	" tripod	"	"	28,531	"	vase	"	"
28,473	"	globular vessel	"	"	28,532	"	" tripod	"	"
28,474	"	small vase	"	"	28,533	"	bowl	"	"
28,475	"	shoe-shaped vessel	"	"	28,534	"	vase	"	"
28,476	"	small vase	"	"	28,535	"	"	"	"
28,477	"	double cup	"	"	28,536	"	bowl	"	"
28,478	"	vase, tripod	"	"	28,537	"	"	"	"
28,479	"	" "	"	"	28,538	"	"	"	"
28,480	"	" "	"	"	28,539	"	vase, tripod	"	"
28,481	"	"	"	"	28,540	"	"	"	"
28,482	"	"	"	"	28,541	"	vessel	"	"
28,483	"	bowl	"	"	28,542	"	"	"	"
28,484	"	vase, tripod	"	"	28,543	"	"	"	"
28,485	"	" "	"	"	28,544	"	"	"	"
28,486	"	bowl	"	"	28,545	"	" shoe-shaped	"	"
28,487	"	"	"	"	28,546	"	" " small,	"	"
28,488	"	"	"	"	28,547	"	"	"	"
28,489	"	vase, tripod	"	"	28,548	"	"	"	"
28,490	"	bowl	"	"	28,549	"	"	"	"
28,491	"	small bowl	"	"	28,550	"	"	"	"
28,492	"	"	"	"	28,551	"	" shoe-shaped	"	"
28,493	(2 Nos.) Pottery bowls		"	"	28,552	"	"	"	"
28,494	Pottery vase, tripod		"	"	28,553	"	"	"	"
28,495	"	"	"	"	28,554	"	" small	"	"
28,496	"	bowl	"	"	28,555	"	" shoe-shaped	"	"
28,497	"	" small	"	"	28,556	"	"	"	"

CATALOGUE OF THE COLLECTION—Continued.

No.	Description				No.	Description			
28,557	Pottery vessel		Santa Helena, Ometepec.		28,616	Pottery vessel, shoe-shaped, Santa Helena, Ometepec.			
28,558	"	"		"	"	28,617	"	"	"	"	"
28,559	"	"		"	"	28,618	"	"		"	"
28,560	"	"		"	"	28,619	"	"		"	"
28,561	"	"		"	"	28,620	"	vase		"	"
28,562	"	"		"	"	28,621	"	vessel, shoe-shaped,	"	"
28,563	"	"		"	"	28,622	"	"		"	"
28,564	"	"		"	"	28,622 (Dup. No.) Pottery vessel		"	"
28,565	"	"		"	"	28,623 Pottery vessel			"	"
28,566	"	"		"	"	28,624	"	" shoe-shaped	"	"
28,567	"	"		"	"	28,625	"	"		"	"
28,568	"	"		"	"	28,626	"	"		"	"
28,569	"	"		"	"	28,627	"	" shoe-shaped	"	"
28,570	"	"		"	"	28,628	"	"		"	"
28,571	"	"		"	"	28,629	"	"		"	"
28,572	"	"		"	"	28,630	"	"		"	"
28,573	"	"		"	"	28,631	"	"		"	"
28,574	"	"		"	"	28,632	"	"		"	"
28,575	"	"		"	"	28,633	"	" shoe-shaped	"	"
28,576	"	"		"	"	28,634	"	"	"	"	"
28,577	"	"		"	"	28,635	"	"	"	"	"
28,578	"	"		"	"	28,636	"	"		"	"
28,579	"	"		"	"	28,637	"	"		"	"
28,580	"	"		"	"	28,638	"	"		"	"
28,581	"	"		"	"	28,639	"	"		"	"
28,582	"	" shoe-shaped	"	"	28,640	"	"		"	"
28,583	"	" small	"	"	28,641	"	"		"	"
28,584	"	" from the mound at Los Cocos, "	28,642	"	"		"	"
28,585	"	" shoe-shaped Santa Helena,	"	28,643	"	"		"	"
28,586	"	"		"	"	28,644	"	"		"	"
28,587	"	"		"	"	28,645	"	"		"	"
28,588	"	"		"	"	28,646	"	"		"	"
28,589	"	"		"	"	28,647	"	"		"	"
28,590	"	"		"	"	28,648	"	" shoe-shaped	"	"
28,591	"	"		"	"	28,649	"	"		"	"
28,592	"	"		"	"	28,650	"	"		"	"
28,593	"	vase		"	"	28,651	"	" shoe-shaped	"	"
28,594	"	bowl		"	"	28,652	"	"	"	"	"
28,595	"	vessel, shoe-shaped,	"	"	28,653	"	"		"	"
28,596	"	"		"	"	28,654	"	" shoe-shaped	"	"
28,597	"	"		"	"	28,655	"	"		"	"
28,598	"	" small	"	"	28,656	"	"		"	"
28,599	"	" shoe-shaped	"	"	28,657	"	"		"	"
28,600	"	"		"	"	28,658	"	"		"	"
28,601	"	" shoe-shaped	"	"	28,659	"	"		"	"
28,602	"	"		"	"	28,660	"	" shoe-shaped	"	"
28,603	"	"		"	"	28,661	"	"	"	"	"
28,604	"	"		"	"	28,662	"	"		"	"
28,605	"	"		"	"	28,663	"	"		"	"
28,606	"	"		"	"	28,664	"	" tripod		"	"
28,607	"	"		"	"	28,665	"	"		"	"
28,608	"	"		"	"	28,666	"	"		"	"
28,609	"	"		"	"	28,667	"	"		"	"
28,610	"	"		"	"	28,668	"	"		"	"
28,611	"	"		"	"	28,669	"	"		"	"
28,612	"	" shoe-shaped	"	"	28,670	"	"		"	"
28,613	"	" "	"	"	28,671	"	"		"	"
28,614	"	"		"	"	28,672	"	"		"	"
28,615	"	"		"	"	28,673	"	"		"	"

CATALOGUE OF THE COLLECTION—Continued.

No.	Description	Locality
28,674	Pottery vessel	Santa Helena, Ometepec.
28,675	" "	" "
28,676	" "	" "
28,677	" "	" "
28,678	" "	" "
28,679	" "	" "
28,680	" " shoe-shaped	" "
28,681	" " " "	" "
28,682	" " " "	" "
28,683	" " " "	" "
28,684	" "	" "
28,685	" "	" "
28,686	" " shoe-shaped	" "
28,687	" "	" "
28,688	" "	" "
28,689	" " small	" "
28,690	" "	" "
28,691	" "	" "
28,692	" "	" "
28,693	" " small, shoe-shaped,	" "
28,694	" " small	" "
28,695	" "	" "
28,696	" "	" "
28,697	" "	" "
28,698	" " shoe-shaped	" "
28,699	" "	" "
28,700	" "	" "
28,701	" "	" "
28,702	" "	" "
28,703	" " shoe-shaped	" "
28,704	" " " "	" "
28,705	" " " "	" "
28,706	" "	" "
28,707	" "	" "
28,708	" "	" "
28,709	" "	" "
28,710	" " bowl	" "
28,711	" " vessel	" "
28,712	" " " "	" "
28,713	" "	" "
28,714	" " shoe-shaped	" "
28,715	" " " "	" "
28,716	" " small	" "
28,717	" "	" "
28,718	" " small, shoe-shaped,	" "
28,719	" " shoe-shaped	" "
28,720	" " small	" "
28,721	" "	" "
28,722	" "	" "
28,723	" " shoe-shaped	" "
28,724	" " bowl	" "
28,725	" " vessel, shoe-shaped,	" "
28,726	" "	" "
28,727	" " shoe-shaped	" "
28,728	" "	" "
28,729	" "	" "
28,730	" "	" "
28,731	" "	" "
28,732	" "	" "
28,733	Pottery vessel	Santa Helena, Ometepec.
28,734	" "	" "
28,735	" "	" "
28,736	" "	" "
28,737	" "	" "
28,737	(Dup. No.) Pottery vessel	" "
28,738	Pottery vessel	" "
28,739	" "	" "
28,740	" "	" "
28,741	" "	" "
28,742	" "	" "
28,743	" "	" "
28,744	" "	" "
28,745	" "	" "
28,746	" "	" "
28,747	" "	" "
28,748	" "	" "
28,749	" "	" "
28,750	" "	" "
28,751	" "	" "
28,752	" "	" "
28,753	" "	" "
28,754	" "	" "
28,755	" "	" "
28,756	" "	" "
28,757	" "	" "
28,758	" "	" "
28,759	" "	" "
28,760	" "	" "
28,761	" "	" "
28,762	" "	" "
28,763	" "	" "
28,764	" "	" "
28,765	" "	" "
28,765	(Dup. No.) Pottery vessel	" "
28,766	Pottery vessel	" "
28,767	" "	" "
28,768	" "	" "
28,769	" "	" "
28,770	" "	" "
28,771	" "	" "
28,772	" "	" "
28,773	" "	" "
28,774	" "	" "
28,775	" "	" "
28,776	" "	" "
28,777	" "	" "
28,778	" "	" "
28,779	" "	" "
28,780	" "	" "
28,781	" "	" "
28,782	" "	" "
28,783	" "	" "
28,784	" "	" "
28,785	" "	" "
28,786	" "	" "
28,787	" "	" "
28,788	" "	" "
28,789	" "	" "

No.	Description	Locality
28,790	Pottery vessel	Santa Helena, Ometepec.
28,791	" "	" "
28,792	" "	" "
28,793	" "	" "
28,794	" "	" "
28,795	" "	" "
28,796	" "	" "
28,797	" "	" "
28,798	" "	" "
28,799	" "	" "
28,800	" "	" "
28,801	" "	" "
28,802	" "	" "
28,803	" "	" "
28,804	" "	" "
28,805	" "	" "
28,806	" "	" "
28,807	" "	" "
28,808	" "	" "
28,809	" "	" "
28,810	" "	" "
28,811	" fragments, sinkers	" "
28,812	" " " (on fisherman's skull)	" "
28,813	Pottery bowl of Luna type	Chilalie, " "
28,814	" oblong urn	" "
28,815	" vessel	" "
28,816	" small painted image, near bowl	" "
28,817	" bowl	" "
28,818	" vase	" "
28,819	" fragment	Los Cocos, " "
28,820	" "	" "
28,821	" "	" "
28,822	" "	" "
28,823	" "	" "
28,824	" "	" "
28,825	Spear-head	mound " "
28,826	Mortar of basalt	near " "
28,827	Flint chips	Santa Helena, " "
28,828	Fragments of implements in basalt	" "
28,829	Flint spear-heads	" "
28,830	Lava sinkers	" "
28,831	Image	" "
28,832	Spear-head	" "
28,833	"	" "
28,834	"	" "
28,835		
28,836	Spear-head	Santa Helena,
28,837	Celt	" "
28,838	"	" "
28,839	Basalt implement	" "
28,840	" pestle	" "
28,841	" " fragment	" "
28,842	" " "	" "
28,843	Stone sinker	" "
28,844	Basalt mortar	" "
28,845	Pestle fragment	" "
28,846	Stone sinker	" "
28,847	Flint chips	Santa Helena, Ometepec.
28,848	" "	" "
28,849	" "	" "
28,850	" "	" "
28,851	" "	" "
28,852	Flint implements, fragments,	" "
28,853	Lava sinker	" "
28,854	" image, broken	" "
28,855	" mortar	" "
28,856	Pottery vase, tripod	" "
28,857	" vessel	" "
28,858	" vase, tripod	" "
28,859	" "	" "
28,860	" vessel	" "
28,861	" "	" "
28,862	" "	" "
28,863	" vase, tripod	" "
28,864	" vessel	" "
28,865	" "	" "
28,866	" beads	Managua, P.
28,867	" fragments	Santa Helena, Ometepec.
28,868	" "	" "
28,869	" "	" "
28,870	" "	" "
28,871	" "	" "
28,872	" "	" "
28,873	" "	" "
28,874	" "	" "
28,875	" "	" "
28,876	" "	" "
28,877	" "	" "
28,878	" "	" "
28,879	" "	" "
28,880	" "	" "
28,881	" cover	" "
28,882	" fragment	" "
28,883	" "	" "
28,884	" "	" "
28,885	" "	" "
28,886	" whistle	" "
28,887	" fragment	" "
28,888	" "	" "
28,889	" "	" "
28,890	" small image	" "
28,891	" "	" "
28,892	" " broken,	" "
28,893	" " "	" "
28,894	" " fragments,	" "
28,895	" " "	" "
28,896	" " "	" "
28,897	" " "	" "
28,898	" spindle whorls	" "
28,899	" perforated discs	" "
28,900	" rattle balls	" "
28,901	" fragments	" "
28,902	" "	" "
28,903	" "	" "
28,904	" "	" "
28,905	" "	" "

CATALOGUE OF THE COLLECTION—Continued.

No.	Description	Locality	
28,906	Pottery fragments	Santa Helena, Ometepec.	
28,907	" "	" "	
28,908	" "	" "	
28,908 (Dup. No.)	Pottery fragments,	" "	
28,909	Pottery fragments	" "	
28,910	" "	" "	
28,911	" sinkers	" "	
28,912	" vase	Palmar, Nicaragua.	
28,913	" cup	" "	
28,914	" vase	" "	
28,915	" "	" "	
28,916	" " Palos Negros, near	" "	
28,917	" "	" "	
28,918	" "	" "	
28,919	" "	" "	
28,920	" "	Sapoa, Costa Rica.	P.
28,921	" "	Los Cocos, Ometepec.	
28,922	" "	Jesus Marin,	"
28,923	" " broken	" "	
28,924	" dish		
28,925	" vessel (modern)	Masaya, Nicaragua.	P.
28,826	" fragments	Palmar, Nicaragua.	
28,927	" "	" "	
28,928	" "	" "	
28,929	" "	" "	
28,930	" vessel (modern)	Masaya, Nicaragua.	P.
28,931	" "	" "	P.
28,932	" "	Nicaragua.	
28,933	" "		
28,934	" "		
28,935	" "		
28,936	" vase, tripod	Managua, Nicaragua.	P.
28,937	" vessel	Aciencia, Costa Rica.	P.
28,938	" " tripod	" "	P.
28,939	" " "	" "	P.
28,940	" "	Rincon,	P.
28,941	" "	" "	P.
28,942	" "	Rincon,	P.
28,943	" " tripod	Culebra,	P.
28,944	" "	" "	P.
28,945	" "	" "	P.
28,946	" "	Bocarones,	P.
28,947	" " tripod	" "	P.
28,948	" "	Nicoya,	"
28,949	" "	" "	
28,950	" "	" "	
28,951	" "	" "	
28,952	" whistle	" "	
28,953	" "	" "	
28,954	" "	" "	P.
28,955	" "	" "	P.
28,956	" "	" "	P.
28,957	" "	Aciencia,	P.
28,958	Pottery cup	Nicoya, Costa Rica.	P.
28,959	" fragment	Culebra,	P.
28,960	" "	Aciencia,	P.
28,961	" "	Nicoya,	P.
28,962	" "	" "	P.
28,963	" "	Aciencia,	P.
28,964	" "	Nicoya,	P.
28,965	" "	" "	P.
28,966	" "	" "	P.
28,967	" "	Nagascola,	P.
28,968	Stone "	Nicoya,	P.
28,969	Image	Aciencia,	P.
28,970	Celt	Nicoya,	P.
28,971	Marine shells from mound at Culebra,		P.
28,972	" " " "		P.
28,973	" " " "		P.
28,974	" " " "		P.
28,975	" " " "		P.
28,976	" " " "		P.
28,977	Green stone ornament (jadeite), Nicoya,		P.
28,978	" amulet	Sardinal,	P.
28,979	" tortoise	"	P.
28,980	" amulet (argillite)	"	P.
28,981	" pendant " "		P.
28,982	" bead (jadeite) "		P.
28,983	" " (argillite), Aciencia,		P.
28,984	" amulet (argillite) Nagascola,		P.
28,985	" " Sardinal,		P.
28,986	" " "		P.
28,987	" amulet (jadeite), Aciencia,		P.
28,988	" " (argillite), "		P.
28,989	" " (jadeite), "		P.
28,990	" " Sardinal,		P.
28,991	" celt (jadeite), Bocarones,		P.
28,992	" fragments (jadeite,) Culebra,		P.
28,993	" " (pebble), Hostianal,		P.
28,994	Fragments—a from burial urn; b and c, a block, Nagascola; the rest from Hostianal		P.
28,995	Curiol	Nicoya, "	P.
28,996		Nicaragua.	
28,997	Oblong urn	Ometepec, "	P.
31,389	Amulet of pottery	Campo Santo, Ometepec.	
32,762	Metate and roller	Palmar, Nicaragua.	
32,763	Terra-cotta bowl, Luna hacienda, Ometepec, "		
32,764	Pottery fragments		"
32,766	" vessel		"
32,767	" spindle whorl		"
32,768	" whistle		"
32,769	" dog, spotted, Santa Helena, Ometepec, "		
32,770	" armadillo " "		"
32,771	" fragments	"	"
32,773	" burial urn, Luna hacienda, "		"

EXPLANATIONS OF PLATE I.

In this plate are given photographs of a few typical forms of pottery objects for the purpose of exhibiting the character of the workmanship, which could not be well represented by the illustrations in the text. The detailed account of each specimen will be found under the corresponding Smithsonian number in the body of the work.

Fig.						
1—	Smith. No. 28,678—⅓ size.	Funeral urn	Santa Helena, Ometepec, Nicaragua
2—	28,447—⅓ "	Toy in Santa Helena terra-cotta	"	"	"
3—	28,730—⅓ "	Earthen vessel	"	"	"
4—	22,394—¹⁄₁₂ "	Burial urn	Luna hacienda,	"	"
5—	22,317—⅙ "	Bowl of Luna terra-cotta	"	"	"
6—	22,360—⅙ "	Deep bowl "	"	"	"
7—	22,375—⅓ "	Vase "	"	"	"
8—	28,460—⅓ "	Pottery of Peruvian style	Santa Helena,	"	"
9—	28,556—⅓ "	Earthen vessel	"	"	"
10—	28,953—⅓ "	Earthen whistle	Nicoya, Costa Rica.
11—	28,905—¼ "	Fragment of funeral urn	Santa Helena, Ometepec, Nicaragua.
12—	28,952—¼ "	Earthen whistle	Nicoya, Costa Rica.
13—	28,908—¼ "	Fragment of funeral urn	Santa Helena, Ometepec, Nicaragua.
14—	28,896—⅓ "	Head of earthen image	"	"	"
15—	23,756—⅙ "	Vessel in black ware	Luna hacienda,	"	"
16—	28,493—¼ "	Vase, Santa Helena terra-cotta	Santa Helena,	"	"
17—	28,483—¼ "	Shallow bowl, "	"	"	"
18—	22,409—⅓ "	Parrot's head, "	Los Angeles,	"	"
19—	28,912—¼ "	Vase	Palmar,	"
20—	28,468—¼ "	Vessel, Santa Helena terra-cotta	Santa Helena, Ometepec,	"
21—	22,345—⅙ "	" black ware	Luna hacienda,	"	"
22—	22,389—⅙ "	" " "	"	"	"
23—	22,366—⅓ "	Bowl, Luna terra-cotta	"	"	"
24—	Gold image; gold, terra-cotta and argillite beads (first line gold, second terra-cotta, third argillite)		"	"	"

EXPLANATIONS OF PLATE II.

Fig.						
1—	Smith. No. 28,982—A little less than ½ size.	Jadeite bead	Sardinal, Costa Rica.
2—	28,987—	"	"	" amulet	Aciencia,	"
3—	28,990—	"	"	" " (fragment)	Sardinal,	"
4—	28,989—	"	"	" "	Aciencia,	"
5—	28,991—	"	"	" celt	Buearones,	"
6—	28,992—	"	"	" fragment	Culebra,	"
7—	28,978—	"	"	Serpentine bird	Sardinal,	"
8—	28,977—	"	"	Jadeite gorget	Nicoya,	"
9—	28,980—	"	"	Argillite amulet	Sardinal,	"
10—	28,984—	"	"	"	Nagascola,	"
11—	28,986—	"	"	"	Sardinal,	"
12—	28,981—	"	"	"	"	"
13—	28,979—	"	"	Green marble turtle	"	"
14—	28,988—	"	"	Argillite amulet	Aciencia,	"
15—	28,983—	"	"	" bead	"	"
16—	28,986—	"	"	" amulet	Sardinal,	"

(93)

INDEX.

Abbott, C. C., 77.
Academy of Natural Sciences, Philadelphia, Proceedings, 1.
Alta Gracia, 6.
Amazon, 81, 82.
Amulets, 75.
Anahuac, 81.
Argillite, 45, 77.
Assyria, 34.
Axes, 51.
Aztec, 4, 7, 46, 58, 78, 79, 80, 82.

Baltaza, Hacienda de, 6, 46.
Bancroft, H. H., 57, 58, 78, 80.
Bastian, A., 81.
Beads, 19, 45, 47.
Berendt, C. H., 4, 46, 56, 79, 81, 82.
Bocarones, 74.
Bogota, 46, 81.
Boyle, 80.
Brazil, 81.
Burial urns, 9, 15, 46, 47, 74, 81.

Calendar stone of Mexico, 58.
Campo Santo, 7, 8, 10, 12, 19.
Canal, Report of Surveys for, 1, 3, 73.
Caribs, 82.
Cartago, 3.
Catherwood, F., 51, 59.
Celt, 53, 75, 77.
Chalchihuitl, 75, 77, 78.
Chalchihuitlicue, 78.
Charcoal, 51.
Chiapas, 62.
Chibchas, 82.
Chilaite, 26, 47, 61.
Chiriqui, 60.
Cholula, 4, 79.
Cholutecas, 4, 79.
Chontales, 80.
Chorotegas, 4, 79, 80, 81.
Cihuacohuatl, 58.
Clavigero, 78.
Cohuatlicue, 58.
Coibas, 46.
Colombia, 46, 81.
Copan, 54, 57.
Costa Rica, 3, 44, 46, 51.
Culebra, Hacienda de, 74, 76, 77.

Culebra Bay, 71.
Curiol, 54, 75.

Dall, W. H., 45, 46.
Dirians, 4.
D'Orbigny, 81.
Dow, J. M., 20, 21, 41, 46.

El Jovo, 73.
Essequibo, 82.

Flint chips, 47, 51.
Flint, Dr. Earl, 46, 70, 72, 76, 77, 80.
Friedrichstahl, 80.
Funeral urns, 51.

Gallatin, A., 58.
Gorget, 75.
Granada, 46.
Guarayos, 81.
Guatemala, 56, 58, 59, 79, 81.
Gugumatz, 59.

Hartt, C. F., 21, 81, 82.
Herrera, 4, 79.
Hostianal, 73.
Huehuetenango, 51, 56.
Huitzilopochtli, 58.
Humboldt, A., 81, 82.
Hurtado, Don David, 73.

Images, gold, 46, 53, 62, 74, 82.
Iztli, 46.

Jadeite, 77.
Jones, Charles C., 81.
Jones, Joseph, 60.

Keller, Franz, 81.
Kingsborough, Lord, 57.
Kukulcan, 59.

La Domiga, 7, 11, 19.
Leon, 4.
Levy, P., 3.
Lopez mine, 7, 14, 19.
Los Angeles, 6, 60, 63.
Los Cocos, 56, 61, 63, 80.
Lull, E. P., Commander, U. S. N., 1, 20.
Luna hacienda, 7, 8, 20.
Luna terra-cotta, 20, 50, 80.

Madera, 5, 44, 63, 82.
Managua, 59, 70, 80, 82.
Marabios, 4.
Marajo, 21.
Martius, Von, 81.
Masaya, 71.
Mason, Prof. O. T., 57.
Maya, 54, 80, 82.
Merritt, Dr. J. King, 60.
Metates, 69, 75.
Mexico, 58, 59, 62, 70, 78, 79, 82.
Monhegan, 70.
Monjas, Casa de, Uxmal, 59.
Mounds, 60, 81.
Moyogalpa, 6, 7.
Muyscas, 52, 82.

Nandaime, 70, 73, 80.
Nagascola, 71, 76.
New Granada (Colombia), 82.
Nicoya, 4, 73, 76, 79.
Nindiri, 80.

Obsidian, 46.
Ocosingo, 34, 80.
Ometepec, 5.
Orinoco, 82.
Orotiñans, 4.
Oviedo, 4, 79, 80.

Palenque, 54, 58.
Palmar, 69.
Palos Negros, 69, 80.
Panama, 81, 82.
Peabody Museum, 20.
Peruvian style of ware, 57.
Piedrahita, 78.
Pipes, absence of, 46.
Plumed serpent, 58.
Pottery, Luna, 20, 50.
    Santa Helena, 20, 50.
    Manufacture of, at San Jorge, 71.
    Manufacture of, among Savage Races, 60.
Pueblo Viejo, 7, 49, 61.
Pumpelly, Prof. Raphael, 77.

Quetzalcoatl, 58, 59.
Quezatlcohuatl, 58.

(95)

Rau, Prof. Charles, 77.
Rivas, 5, 46, 79.
Rock inscriptions, 64, 82.

Sacrificial stone of Mexico, 58.
Sahagun, 78.
Saffray, 78.
San Francisco, 59.
San Jorge, 71.
San Juan del Sur, 70, 73.
San Ramon, Point, 64.
Santa Helena, 60, 61, 80.
Santa Helena terra-cotta, 14, 47, 50, 55.
Sapos, 3, 73.
Sardinal, 73, 77.
Sawfish, teeth of, 54.
Schomburk, Sir R. H., 82.
Schoolcraft, H. R., 70.

Seemann, B., 82.
Serpent symbol, 34.
Shark, vertebra of, 50, 54.
Shell-heaps, 51, 71, 76.
Shells, 46.
Shoe-shaped vessels, 51, 61.
Simon, 78.
Sinkers, 51.
Sivers, 50, 82.
Soconusco, 79.
Spear heads, 51, 53.
Squier, E. G., 34, 47, 58, 59, 64, 77, 78, 82.
Stephens, J. L,, 51, 56, 57.
Stone grave, 59, 81.
St. Thomas, 82.

Tempisque, 3, 4, 73, 74.

Teotihuacan, 57.
Ternaux-Compans, 78.
Tiahuanuco, 82.
Tierra Blanca, 63.
Torquemada, 4, 79.

Urn burial, 7. *See* Burial urns.
Uxmal, 59.

Virgin Bay, 73.

Whistle, 54, 75.
Whitfield, Dr. B. H., 73.

Young, Miss, 81.
Yucatan, 59, 62.

Zapatera, 74, 80.
Zeledon, Don José, 4.

PLATE I.

POTTERY AND ORNAMENTS FROM NICARAGUA.

PLATE II.

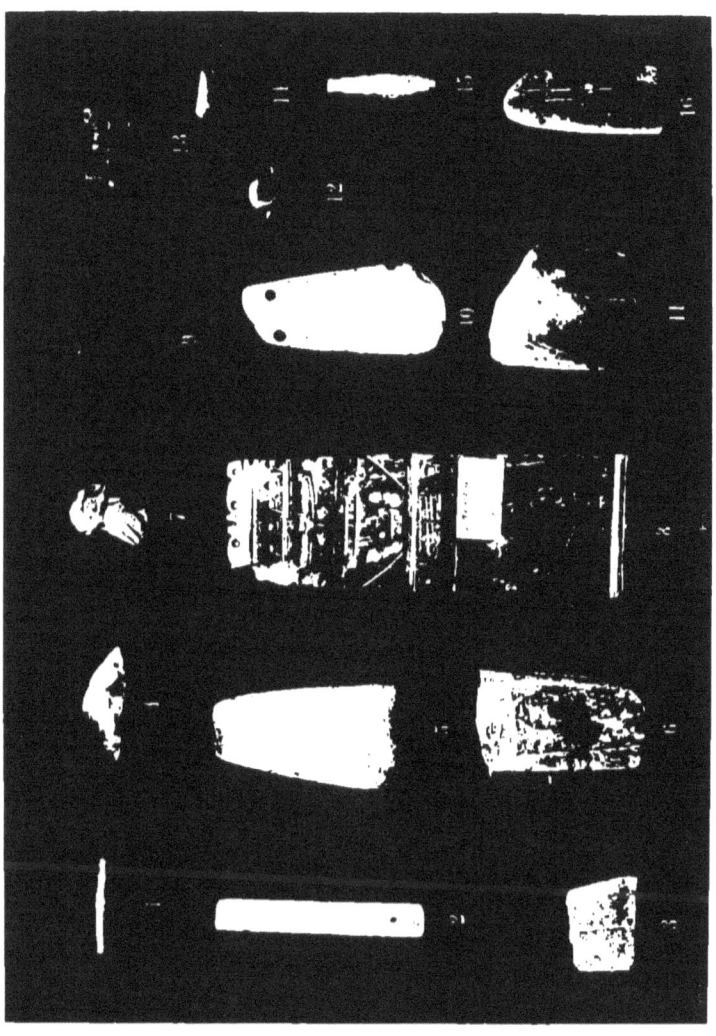

www.ingramcontent.com/pod-product-compliance
Lightning Source LLC
Chambersburg PA
CBHW030907170426
43193CB00009BA/764